Iran's
Foreign Policy

From **Khatami** to **Ahmadinejad**

Iran's Foreign Policy

From **Khatami** to **Ahmadinejad**

Edited by

Anoushiravan Ehteshami and Mahjoob Zweiri

ITHACA
PRESS

IRAN'S FOREIGN POLICY
From Khatami to Ahmadinejad

Published by
Ithaca Press
8 Southern Court
South Street
Reading
Berkshire
RG1 4QS
UK
www.ithacapress.co.uk

Ithaca Press is an imprint of Garnet Publishing Limited

First Edition

ISBN-13: 978-0-86372-324-7

British Library Cataloguing-in-Publication Data
A catalogue record for this book is available from the British Library

Typeset by Samantha Barden
Jacket design by David Rose
Cover photo used with permission Atta Kenare/AFP/Getty Images

Printed in Lebanon

Contents

Preface

The controversy over Iran's foreign policy is as old as the Islamic Republic itself. One of the new regime's main contributions to it was the revolutionary elite's insistence that its main principle is 'neither East nor West'. The dynamics of Iran's foreign policy and the constant changes in the state's conduct have encouraged academics to try to understand its policy and to put its international relations in a wider perspective. Their publications have covered different aspects of Iranian foreign policy and its development under various administrations. But the complexities of modern Iran and its international environment are such that we believe there is still much more research to be undertaken.

In view of this, we consider that the Khatami era provides a fascinating test case of the changes taking place in Iran's foreign relations. Thus in 2002, we began preparing for a major international conference that would explore the various aspects of the Khatami administration's unique foreign policy.

The aim of this conference, held at Durham University in March 2005, was to discuss specific themes in Iran's foreign policy by bringing together leading academics and political figures from Iran and other parts of the world. The various themes we wanted to explore were familiar ones: ideology, domestic politics, Iranian foreign policy in action, Iranian foreign policy and conflict zones in the Middle East, Iran and Europe and Iranian foreign policy and the United States.

The conference discussed the changes that Iran's foreign policy had undergone since 1997 and, more specifically, since the 2003 parliamentary elections, and it looked at the possible developments in its policy that the country would face after the ninth presidential elections in June 2005. During this two-day conference, 21 papers were presented by first-class academics and experts. The discussion covered the above themes from different perspectives and included the latest analysis of the attitudes, implications and consequences of Iranian foreign policy for the international community. This book includes the papers, many of which have since been fully updated, that addressed the main themes of the conference.

We are very grateful to our contributors for their hard work in producing these inspired papers for the collection and also to our publisher for ensuring that the book reaches the market so soon after its completion. We hope that the contents, views and analysis of this book will open the door for further dialogue and debate on the foreign policy of Iran, especially given the rapid changes taking place in Iran itself if not the Middle East more broadly.

Anoush Ehteshami and Mahjoob Zweiri
Durham, June 2007

Contributors

Michael Axworthy visited Iran many times in the 1970s as a teenager, travelling around the country extensively. In the 1980s, he studied history at Peterhouse, Cambridge before joining the Foreign and Commonwealth Office (FCO) in 1986. He served as Head of the Iran Section at the FCO from 1998 to 2000, which coincided with the improvement in UK–Iran relations at the beginning of the presidency of Muhammad Khatami. He left the FCO in 2000, and his first book, *The Sword of Persia*, about the great Iranian conqueror Nader Shah, was published in July 2006. He has also written articles on Iran and other subjects for *Prospect* magazine and made TV appearances in which he has discussed the Iran nuclear crisis. Since October 2005, he has taught Middle Eastern history at the Institute of Arab and Islamic Studies at the University of Exeter, where he is an honorary fellow and is working on a general history of Iran.

Anastasia Drenou received a BA in history and international relations from the American College of Thessaloniki in Greece and an MSc (Res.) in Islamic and Middle Eastern studies from the University of Edinburgh. She is a PhD candidate at the School of History at the University of St Andrews in Scotland. Her thesis examines the relations between the European Union and the Islamic Republic of Iran since 1979.

Anoushiravan Ehteshami is Professor of International Relations and Head of the School of Government and International Affairs at Durham University. He is also a fellow of the World Economic Forum. He was Vice President of the British Society for Middle Eastern Studies from 2000 to 2003.

His many book-length publications include *Globalization and Geopolitics in the Middle East: Old Games, New Rules* (New York: Routledge, 2007); *Iran and the Rise of its Neoconservatives: The Politics of Tehran's Silent Revolution* (with Mahjoob Zweiri) (London: I.B. Tauris, 2007);

and *The Middle East's Relations with Asia and Russia* (co-editor) (London: RoutledgeCurzon, 2004).

His current research concentrates on five themes: the Asian balance of power in the post-Cold War era; the international politics of the Red Sea subregion; the foreign and security policies of Middle Eastern states after the Cold War; the impact of globalization on the Middle East; and governance and efforts at democratization in the Middle East.

R.K. Ramazani is Edward R. Stettinius Professor Emeritus of Government and Foreign Affairs at the University of Virginia, where he has been based since 1952. He is a founder of Iranian foreign policy studies in the United States and has authored and edited 15 books and more than 150 articles on Iran, the Persian Gulf and the Middle East. He is a veteran member of the editorial board of *The Middle East Journal* and other scholarly journals concerned with the Middle East. He has been consulted by the US departments of State, Defence and the Treasury and by the United Nations.

Ali Akbar Rezaei serves as Director of the North America Department at the Ministry of Foreign Affairs of Iran. He joined the Institute for Political and International Studies (IPIS), which is affiliated to the Iranian foreign ministry, as a researcher in 1998. He became Head of the Strategic Programme at IPIS in 2000, before serving as the representative of IPIS in London from 2001 to 2005.

Christopher Rundle is a graduate of Cambridge University. After a year at the Central Asian Research Centre in London, he joined the Foreign Office in 1963. He was posted to Tehran both before and after the revolution and to Afghanistan. In London, he was a research counsellor with responsibility mainly for Iranian affairs. He has travelled widely in the Middle East and Afghanistan.

Since retiring in 1998, he has been an honorary fellow of Durham University, and he is Honorary President of its Centre for Iranian Studies. He is also on the advisory council of the British Institute of Persian Studies. His memoirs, *From Colwyn Bay to Kabul: an Unexpected Journey*, were published in 2004.

Shahriar Sabet-Saeidi is Assistant Director of the Institute of Iranian Studies at the University of St Andrews in Scotland. He is a PhD candidate at Durham University and has an MA in Middle Eastern politics from Durham University and an LLB from Shahid Beheshti University in Tehran.

Judith S. Yaphe is Distinguished Research Fellow at the Institute for National Strategic Studies (INSS) at the National Defense University (NDU) in Washington, DC. She specialises in Iraq, Iran and Persian Gulf security issues. Before joining the INSS in 1995, Dr Yaphe was a senior political analyst in the Office of Near Eastern–South Asian Analysis at the Central Intelligence Agency, where she received the Intelligence Medal of Commendation for her work on Iraq. Her recent research has focused on the impact of American policy on Iraq, Iran and the wider Gulf region. Her latest publications include *Reassessing the Implications of a Nuclear-Armed Iran* (McNair Paper 69, NDU, 2005); *Turbulent Transition in Iraq: Can It Succeed?* (Strategic Forum 208, 2004); *Political Reconstruction in Iraq: A Reality Check* (Carnegie Institute for International Peace, 2003); and *The Strategic Implications of a Nuclear-Armed Iran* (McNair Paper 64, NDU, 2001).

Dr Yaphe received a BA with honours in history from Moravian College in Pennsylvania and a PhD in Middle Eastern history from the University of Illinois.

Mahjoob Zweiri is a specialist in Middle Eastern politics and Iran. He was a research fellow at the Institute for Middle Eastern and Islamic Studies at the University of Durham before becoming Teaching Fellow in Middle East Politics and Director of its Centre for Iranian Studies. He now works for the Centre for Strategic Studies at the University of Jordan as a senior researcher in Middle Eastern and Iranian Affairs.

His research interests include the modern history of the Middle East, political Islam, Arab–Iranian relations, Shi'ism and current developments in Iran. His recent publications include (with Anoushiravan Ehteshami) *Iran and the Rise of Its Neoconservatives: The Politics of Tehran's Silent Revolution* (London: I.B. Tauris, 2007).

Introduction

Anoushiravan Ehteshami and Mahjoob Zweiri

Three central issues dominate debate on the Islamic Republic of Iran (IRI): the nature of the Iranian political system, how the Iranian regime views the Other and the foreign policy that has been in effect since 1979.

In order to gain a better understanding of Iran it is important to analyse its foreign policy. On the one hand, this is the way through which we can assess the relationship between religion and politics in the Islamic Republic and, on the other hand, it is important to understand the impact of Iranian foreign policy on Middle Eastern and international security.

According to the IRI's constitution, Iranian foreign policy is crafted according to four fundamental principles: first, rejection of all forms of external domination; second, preservation of Iran's independence and territorial integrity; third, defence of the rights of all Muslims without allying with hegemonic powers; and, fourth, the maintenance of peaceful relations with all non-belligerent states.

These principles have guided Iranian foreign policy since the Islamic revolution. Nevertheless, a pragmatic approach has been adopted by decision-makers in Iran, and this tends to be driven by regional and international developments. In the light of these principles, it is easy to understand the Islamic Republic's foreign policy and its support for Islamic resistance movements around the world. Also, they make clearer the so-called concept of exporting the revolution, widely advocated by many of those decision-makers in the 1980s.

It can be argued that Iran's endeavours to portray itself as the heart of the Muslim world is an attempt to gain worldwide Muslim support, which gives it more legitimacy in the face of regional and international challenges. However, the principles that guide Iranian foreign policy have created 'enemies of Islam and Iran', as the Islamic Republic regards the West in general and the United States in particular. This animosity has led to the current confrontation between Iran and Western powers because the United States and some European countries consider Iran and its foreign policy to be 'the greatest threat to security and stability in the Middle East'. At crucial junctures, this animosity has tended to dominate the Islamic Republic's relations with the West. There is a widely held belief among Iranians that the backing Iraq received from the West during the Iran–Iraq war in the 1980s was due to the Islamic nature of the Iranian regime.

In this context, it is not too difficult to understand why Iranians have tried to shift their partnerships towards the East. This can be perceived as a response to the cultural attack on the basic principles of the Islamic revolution and to the notorious history of British and American intervention in Iran in the twentieth century, in particular the US-backed overthrow of Prime Minister Muhammad Musaddiq, who as early as the 1950s wanted to nationalize Iran's oil industry.

The majority of Iranian politicians believe that moving towards the East is less risky than building relations with the West, with its hegemonic tendencies. Thus Iran considers China to be a model that should be followed. Leading figures in the Iranian political system, Khamenei, Rafsanjani and Ahmadinejad, have all embraced this belief.

Furthermore, Iran has been moving rapidly towards Latin America and Africa, succeeding in building strong relations with a number of Latin American and African countries, including Cuba and Venezuela. By pursuing such a policy, Iranian policy-makers are not only aiming to strengthen the economy but also trying to alleviate the pressures put on them by the West and the United States.

The Iranian political elite can be divided into four main groups: classics, conservatives, reformists and neoconservatives. Almost all Iranian politicians, except for a group of reformists, agree on the above-mentioned principles. That group believes that it is necessary to maintain relations with the West, arguing that Iranian foreign policy is distorting Iran's image. For this reason, they call for a serious review of Iranian foreign policy.

Over the eight years that preceded Ahmadinejad's coming to power in 2005, Muhammad Khatami's foreign policy was driven mostly by two goals: to create strong links between domestic issues and foreign policy and to improve Iran's relations with the world through a policy of détente and mutual respect.

Khatami was successful in improving the image of both the ayatollahs and Iran. The new, positive impression of the Islamic Republic helped it to gain a more prominent status and to play a more influential role in the Middle East and beyond. By 2001, Khatami's initiative, the Dialogue among Civilizations, had bestowed much respect upon Iran and its president. The new, relaxed atmosphere helped to replace the prevailing belief that Iranian foreign policy was 'closely connected to – and indeed an extension of – policies and priorities of the theocratic regime and its dominant elite'.

What Khatami did was perceived as a 'radical change' in Iranian foreign policy. This change had a deep impact on Iran's relations with a number of European countries, such as France, Spain, Greece and Italy. As a result, he was the first Iranian president to be received in those countries since the 1979 revolution.

The ninth presidential election, in June 2005, brought to power a new Iranian leadership that did not follow in the footsteps of Khatami. Mahmoud Ahmadinejad decided to pursue with more vigour the Eastern shift and the Third World-first policies originally articulated in the 1980s. Also, he revived the fiery rhetoric against Israel and launched a major campaign of Holocaust denial, initiatives and views that had almost completely disappeared during Khatami's presidency.

Iranian foreign policy under Ahmadinejad has proved to be a constant source of tension on both the regional and international levels. In a very direct fashion, the rapid political developments in the domestic arena have spilled over into Iran's foreign policy and regional relations. Questions about Ahmadinejad's foreign policy decision-making are of course valid, but the complexity of decision-making in Iran and the relationship between its power centres could easily lead to a misunderstanding of the Iranian political system.

As with previous Iranian presidents, we can see that although Ahmadinejad has executive authority to pursue Iran's relations with the rest of the world, that authority is still limited. This limitation of authority in the international arena has manifested itself in, for example, Ayatollah Khamenei's appointment of the former foreign affairs minister Dr Kamal Kharrazi as the head of a new foreign policy advisory committee, which is accountable directly to the Supreme Leader's office, not to the president.

The complexity of the Iranian political system and also its foreign policy-making machinery is a constant source of fascination for us. Thus we are keen to follow and shed light on the workings of Iran's foreign relations. This book is an attempt to assess the foreign policy of the former president Khatami and the major changes in Iran's foreign policy under President Ahmadinejad. It has nine chapters.

The first chapter, 'Iran's Foreign Policy: Independence, Freedom and the Islamic Republic', explores the principles, noted above, of the Iranian revolution, which Iranian leaders have variously invoked and interpreted ever since the revolution. The chapter uses a historical approach and framework in understanding Iranian foreign policy. Although it raises more questions and uncertainties than it can resolve, it nonetheless provides a fascinating historical and cultural context to the evolution of Iranian foreign policy.

'Foreign Policy Theories: Implications for the Foreign Policy Analysis of Iran' is the second chapter. It explores the debate over how Iran's foreign policy should be explained and how predictable its foreign policy behaviour is. In particular, it looks at the development of Iranian foreign policy over the past fifty years, taking into consideration the impact on it of the 1979 revolution. The chapter also raises various questions: what should one know about Iran's foreign policy? How does Iran define its interests and choose to pursue them? Is its policy based on words or deeds, behaviour or action? Are the causes or the effects of Iran's foreign policy to be addressed? Are its variables subjective or objective? Are they material or ideational? What is the influence on it of culture? Is it scientific at all to talk about Iran's 'foreign policy'? And can there be a theory or a model of it?

Chapter 3, 'The United States and Iran in Iraq: Risks and Opportunities', puts the United States and Iran in the context of what has materialized in Iraq and the Persian Gulf region since the fall of Saddam Hussein. Its particular focus is the American and Iranian roles in Iraq and the risks and opportunities that have arisen for both actors there and in the region as a whole. In addition, it provides a unique insight into Iraqi perspectives on the role of America and Iran in Iraq. The risks and opportunities for the US government are examined and policy recommendations are made that would help it to minimize risks and maximize opportunities in Iraq and the Gulf.

The fourth chapter is entitled 'Iranian–European Relations: A Strategic Partnership?' It explores the development of relations between Iran and the EU between 1990 and 2005. It reviews Iran's relations with the EU since the presidency of Rafsanjani and studies Europe's response, scrutinizing the idea that Europe is Iran's strategic partner in the West and that this partnership makes it possible for Iran to confront US ambitions in the Middle East.

The chapter finds that Europe can be a strategic partner for Iran with a significant political and economic role but that this would materialize only if Iran enjoyed equal relations with the United States. Owing to its poor relations with the United States, Iran is not yet able to enjoy strategically and decisively the economic, technological and political advantages that accrue from its relations with Europe, and it needs to take into account Europe's limitations in the American-designed new international order.

'Iran: Caught Between European Union–United States Rivalry?', Chapter 5, investigates the background and developments of the 'dual containment' policy adopted by the United States towards Iran and also the Iranian nuclear programme until the end of 2004. It reviews the stance of the European Union towards both. The chapter also demonstrates that regardless of its policies, Iran has been used in a prolonged 'rivalry' between the United States and the European Union on the international stage.

The sixth chapter, 'Iran–United Kingdom Relations since the Revolution: Opening Doors', documents the relationship between Iran and the United Kingdom since the revolution and especially addresses the various obstacles that have affected this. It argues that there has been a genuine change in relations between the two countries. This gives optimism for the future – disagreements are likely to continue between Iran and the United Kingdom, but given the solid foundations upon which relations have been built, difficulties are likely to be overcome, opening the door for further improvement in their diplomatic relations.

Chapter 7, 'Diplomatic Relations Between Iran and the United Kingdom in the Early Reform Period, 1997–2000', gives a general overview of those relations from the election of President Khatami in 1997 to the summer of 2000. It is based on a personal account of how relations between the Iranian and British governments changed in the early Khatami era. In addition to setting out the essential facts of relations between the two countries, the chapter focuses on their motives and intentions and tries to draw out new insights about the effects of internal political developments in Iran and of Iran's international isolation in the 1980s.

The chapter analyses the perceived improvement in relations between the Iranian and British governments after the election of President Khatami, and particularly after statements by the two governments addressing the Rushdie problem in September 1998. It considers the range of policy matters discussed between the two governments, giving due weight to the influence of EU policy. Britain's perception of Iran's intentions and constraints is discussed, as are some of the problems that arose between the two governments over this period and their joint achievements.

The eighth chapter, 'Arab–Iranian Relations: New Realities?', explores the impact of what it calls the new realities in Iran's foreign relations. Developments such as Iran's nuclear programme and the Iraq war and its consequences are considered in the context of Iranian politics and the rise of the neoconservatives to executive power in Iran. It argues that these realities have overshadowed Arab–Iranian relations. The impact of these new realities on the Middle East and their consequences are also discussed.

The final chapter, 'Iran and its Immediate Neighbourhood', attempts to provide an overview of Iran's interactions with its immediate environment. Tracing the priorities of successive administrations in Tehran, it is keen to explore and understand the nature of forces affecting the Persian Gulf sub-region's security paradigms. The chapter pays particular attention to the impact on the wider region of the fall of Baghdad in April 2003 to American-led military forces. With an eye on the evolution of Iranian–Iraqi relations, particularly since regime change in Iraq, it explores the changing nature of the regional dynmaics which have impacted Tehran's regional role perception, and the consequences of this for the republic's foreign policy. It concludes that given the geopolitical realities following regime change in Iraq, the most decisive regional triangle to understand today is the one that ties Iraq to both Iran and the United States.

1

Iran's Foreign Policy:
Independence, Freedom and the Islamic Republic

R.K. Ramazani

Gar az basit-e zamin aql mon'adem gardad gaman nabarad hichkas keh nadanam. [If reason were banished from the face of the earth, no one would imagine himself ignorant.]

Sa'di (1184–1291)

Focusing on the foreign policy of Iran since the revolution of 1979 is most topical. At no time since then has Iran been under such a threat of military action by the United States and Israel for its alleged nuclear weapons ambitions and the nature and principles of its regime. All revolutions declare their guiding ideals, creeds or principles at one time or another and in one form or another. Thus the Americans declared 'unalienable rights' to 'life, liberty and the pursuit of happiness' and the French proclaimed their commitment to 'liberty, equality and fraternity'.

At the dawn of the Iranian revolution, Ayatollah Ruhollah Khomeini called for 'independence, freedom and the Islamic Republic'. This became a rallying cry of the revolution; but unlike the slogan 'Neither East nor West but the Islamic Republic', which lost its meaning after the end of the Cold War, Khomeini's declaration of principles has persisted to the present. Indeed, these principles are embodied in the Iranian Constitution. Iranian leaders have variously invoked and interpreted them ever since the revolution, and Muhammad Khatami when president designated them as 'eternal' (*javidan*).

I hypothesize that these principles have deep roots in Iranian history and culture – since the birth of the Iranian state in ancient times – despite their permutations over more than two millennia. Also, I propose that exploring these principles in the historical and cultural context might deepen our understanding of the dynamic interaction between Iran's domestic and foreign policies since the revolution and aid our thinking about them in the future.

Cicero would have endorsed this historical approach. He said, 'To be ignorant of what happened before you were born is to remain always a child', and Winston Churchill believed that 'The further you look backward, the further forward you can see.' I am fully aware of the pitfalls involved in the kind of probing I intend to do because the further back we go in history, the more uncertainties and perplexities abound. My exploration is thus bound to generate more questions than answers. But this is exactly why I venture into the subject, for much ground remains to be broken by scholars, especially those of the younger generation.

Pre-Islamic Principles

The quest for independence and freedom and their progressive meta-morphosis into major ideals and then principles in the Iranian world view are as old as the Iranian state, founded by Cyrus (558–530 BC). The nascent state expanded within 30 years into the Achaemenid Empire, which lasted for 200 years. Territorially, it stretched from the Nile and the Aegean to the Indus and from the deserts of Africa to the ice-bound borders of China. Demographically, it represented 'the first deliberate attempt in history' to unite heterogeneous peoples from all these territories into a single organized international society, which, we are told by Adda B. Bozeman, the renowned international historian, 'constituted, an important precedent in the history of international peace and organization'. Furthermore, she tells us that the earliest Persian statesmen posed 'for the first time in historically human terms the problems of moral principle in international relations'. Cyrus kept his empire peaceful at a time when 'the tyranny of empires plagued the fabric of community life everywhere'. The fundamental reason for Cyrus's ability to do this was his prudent and tolerant statecraft rather than his religious ethics. He allowed the religious laws of conquered peoples such as the Egyptians, the Babylonians and the Hebrews to remain in force, as testified by Herodotus and Xenophon; and, as is well known, the Bible praises him for liberating the Jews from Babylonian captivity.

However, these notions of independence and freedom were not realized by the Iranians themselves because, starting with Darius I

(522–486 BC), the succeeding Achaemenid and then Sassanid kings arrogated to themselves something like the divine right of kings. Darius declared, 'I am king. Ahura Mazda gave me the kingdom.' This kingly claim to heavenly blessing, called *khavarn* (*farr* in modern Persian), became from then on a major feature of Iranian history and political culture, and the concepts of independence and freedom were subordinated to the sovereignty of the shah as the defender of both religion and the kingdom. Darius also declared that 'I am a friend to right, I am not a friend to wrong'; and on this basis he would reward the right and punish the wrong. But as the dispenser of justice, he demanded absolute loyalty from the people.

The sacred character of the king was clearly postulated on the basis of the Avesta, the scripture of the Zoroastrian faith, during the Sassanid Empire (AD 224–651), founded by Ardashir I (AD 224–39). He claimed divine qualities, and counselled his son in his political testament to 'Consider the altar and the throne as inseparable; they must always sustain one another. A sovereign without religion is a tyrant.' This concept of the close ties between the king and religion was, as will be seen, bequeathed to the Safavid kings, and has been claimed often by Iranian leaders to the present time.

In practice, however, sovereignty and tyranny went together and this became one of the most enduring features of Iranian governance. Religion was used to legitimize and consolidate political power domestically and to justify wars, primarily against Rome and Byzantium. The war against Byzantium in AD 627 is a noteworthy example of all subsequent wars. Iran's disastrous defeat on the battlefield at that time took place during the rule of Khosro II (AD 591–628), who was forced by Heraclius to give up conquered territories. This defeat ushered in a period of great instability, which prepared the way for the conquest of the Sassanid Empire by Muslim armies after the battles of Qadisiyya (AD 636) and Nihavand (AD 642).

Ironically, the Iranian people's sense of cultural identity, rooted in their consciousness of a common origin, in a shared religion and especially in one language, survived the Arab and all other invasions, occupations and material and human devastations and conversion to Islam that followed. Three hundred years after the Arab invasion, that sense of identity found its most eloquent expression in the everlasting heroic epics of Ferdowsi: 'May I not live if Iran liveth not' (*Cho Iran nabashad tan-e man mabad*). He also said that over 30 years, he had resurrected the Iranians by purging Arabic from the Persian language (*ajam zendeh kardam bedin parsi*).

Islamic-era Principles

The concepts of independence and freedom under the Safavid Empire (1502–1722) resembled those of the Sassanids to a striking extent. Just as the Sassanids had 'Zoroastrianized' the empire, so the Safavids 'Shiitized' theirs. The Sassanid idea of close ties between 'throne' and 'altar', that is kingship and religion, was passed to the Safavids. That idea survived during the entire pre-nationalist era, when the king's relation to the people was characterized as the one between 'shepherd' and 'chattel' (*ra'i/ra'iyyat* or *choopan* and *rameh*).

In practice then the Safavids used Shiism for over 200 years primarily to legitimize and consolidate political power rather than to provide freedom for the people. They used it also to justify incessant and inconclusive wars against perceived foreign enemies, particularly the Sunni Ottoman Empire. The purpose of these wars was primarily territorial: either to recover lost territories or to gain new ones. The effects of these wars on the Safavid Empire, combined with ancient problems of social incoherence, political factionalism, corruption of the royal house, fratricide and petrified interpretations of religion, contributed to the ignominious collapse of the empire in 1722. The Iranian state and society did not recover until the early nineteenth century. Nadir Shah's expansionist wars and the rise and fall of the mini-dynastic governments that followed them weakened Iran further. At the turn of the nineteenth century, Iran became sucked into the whirlwind of European imperial rivalries.

Nationalist–Democratic Principles

The historical processes of the nineteenth and early twentieth centuries revolutionized the pre-modern ideas of independence and freedom in Iran, transforming them into the principles of national and democratic independence and freedom. Three processes in particular underpinned this historic metamorphosis: the imposition of reduced international boundaries by foreign powers, the semi-colonization of the state and society and, above all, the flowering of reformist, modernist and secular nationalist and democratic thought.

The treaties that ended the European wars against Iran resulted in a significant diminution of Iranian territory. The most important of these were the treaties of Gulistan (1813) and Turkmanchay (1828) with Russia, the Erzerum treaties of 1823 and 1847 with the Ottoman Empire and the Paris treaty of 1856 with Britain. The territories lost were mostly in Armenia and Transcaucasia.

While imperial Iranian territory was being whittled down, Britain extracted many economic and commercial concessions that transformed Iran into a semi-colonized country in reality if not in name. The major concessionary contracts included the telegraph concessions of 1863–5, the Reuter concession of 1872, the Karun River and Bank concessions of 1888–9 and, in 1901, an oil concession, the first ever granted to a foreign power. Russia too penetrated the Iranian state and society by extracting concessions, including one in 1889 for railway construction and one for non-Persian Gulf custom houses and their revenues in lieu of payment of loans extended to the shah for foreign travel.

The most significant foreign concession of all was the tobacco concession acquired by Britain in 1890. This gave it monopoly control of Iranian tobacco and its products for a projected half-century, and the prospective British company would have the right to sell those products in Iran and also to export them. The shah's government in turn would force Iranian producers to sell their products to the British monopoly. The concession pushed into the open the people's years of accumulated grievances over injurious foreign-imposed treaties and concessions and led to the historic tobacco protest movement of 1891–2.

This protest and the Constitutional Revolution of 1905–11 together brought to the surface an underlying intellectual renaissance, which transformed the Persian–Islamic concepts of independence and freedom for the first time in Iran's long history. Essential to this transformation were the new meanings attached to the concepts of 'nation' (*vatan*) and 'people' (*millat*) by both secular nationalist–democratic and Islamic reformist ideas and ideals.

The controversial secular thinker Mirza Malkam Khan emphasized the overriding importance of man-made law (*qanun*) and its compatibility with Islamic law (sharia). But in effect, he was basing independence and freedom on state law. Sayyed Hasan Taqizadeh did the same by defining *vatan* as the 'human birthplace and residence' (*zadgah va maskan-e ensan*), stressing the concept of liberty and positing that it is compatible with justice. Others argued that love of country and love of religion were compatible on the basis of the Prophet Muhammad's well-known aphorism that 'the love of *vatan* is of faith' (*Hubb al-vatan min al-iman*).

By contrast, the religious activist Jamal al-Din Afghani (Asad-abadi) emphasized the notion of the Muslim people (*millat-i Islamiyyah*), and thus his concepts of independence and freedom from domination by the West, particularly Britain and Russia, extended to the Muslim world as well as Iran.

Afghani's Islamic outlook and values and Malkam's nationalist–democratic ideas and ideals both influenced the historic tobacco protest movement. Afghani's well-known letter of June 1891 to Hajji Mirza Hasan Shirazi induced Shirazi to issue the decree (fatwa) that forbade the people to use tobacco until the British monopoly concession was cancelled, which it was. This show of independence by the long destitute and oppressed people of Iran was unprecedented in its millennial history. It transformed both in practice and in theory the age-old Persian–Islamic concepts of independence and freedom. It also prepared the ground for the subsequent elevation and institutionalization of the concepts of independence and freedom by their inclusion in Iran's first constitution, of 1906–7, as a cardinal principle (*asl*) of Iran's modern world view.

Empowered by the Constitution, the people's representatives in the Parliament (Majlis) decided, among other things, to regulate important economic policies, to manage the budget, to control the transfer of all national resources to foreign powers and to conclude international treaties and conventions. The first Majlis rejected the government's proposal for acquiring foreign loans, protested against the Anglo-Russian convention of 1907 for partitioning Iran into spheres of influence, and hired the American financial adviser Morgan Shuster to help reform Iran's chaotic finances. Praising the representatives of this Majlis, E.G. Brown, the renowned British historian of Iran's constitutional era, said that the deputies 'were animated by a patriotism and public spirit which would have been creditable in the members of any parliament whether in Europe or America'.

Anti-Democratic and Democratic Principles

The rules of Reza Shah (1925–41) and his son Muhammad Reza Shah (1941–79) were essentially anti-democratic. The Pahalvi monarchs cloaked their authoritarian regimes with pre-Islamic conceptions in modern secular garb. Reza Shah's drive for independence helped to stabilize Iran's international boundaries and to abolish the century-old regime of capitulations, but his extension of the British oil concession harmed the Iranian economy for decades before the Anglo-Iranian Oil Company was nationalized as a result of the nationalist–democratic movement led by Prime Minister Muhammad Musaddiq.

Musaddiq's conception of independence and freedom drew from the Constitutional era. Freedom, he insisted, meant that the shah should 'reign, not rule', and independence meant freedom from foreign domination. The era of his rise to power was called 'the revival of the Constitutional period' (*ehya-ye mashrootiyyat*). The basic goal of the nationalist–democratic movement was the same as that of the tobacco protest and the constitutional movements: the end of tyranny and foreign domination.

Musaddiq viewed the choice for Iran as being between 'enslavement and independence' (*enqiad ya esteqlal*), and he believed that social and political reforms would be meaningless as long as Iran's oil industry, the backbone of its economy, was controlled by foreign powers, whether British or Russian. For this reason, he called for the 'nationalization of the oil industry throughout the country' (*melli shodan san'at-e naft dar sarasar-e keshvar*). Many of the ideas and ideals of today's religious and secular reformists are influenced by those of the era of the Constitutional Revolution and the Musaddiq-led nationalist–democratic movement that resulted in the nationalization of the Iranian oil industry in 1951.

After the coup against the Musaddiq government in 1953 the dictatorial rule of the shah expanded. It led to an extravagant version of Iranian independence centred on the shah, and freedom did not see the light of day. Styling himself as Arya Mehr (the light of the Aryans), Muhammad Reza Shah armed Iran to the teeth, to make it one of the five leading conventional military powers of the world. He aspired to an undefined ambitious ideal of the 'Great Civilization' and called his White Revolution first a 'revolution' of the shah and then a 'revolution' of the people. The status-of-forces agreement he signed with the United States (1964) amounted in effect to a return of the privileges of foreign

[7]

capitulations in Iran. Ayatollah Khomeini called it 'the document for the enslavement of Iran'. One of the most popular revolutionary slogans said it all – 'the American shah'.

Revolutionary Principles

Khomeini's concept of independence stemmed from the fundamental premise of his world view: Islam was to serve the ultimate goal of the salvation of humanity. In his words, 'Islam has come for humanity . . . Islam wishes to bring all of humanity under the umbrella of its justice.' As such, the independence of the Muslim community (umma) took priority over that of Iran as a modern nation-state. But that notion differed from the outlook of the religious reformist provisional Prime Minister Mehdi Bazargan, who said that he accorded first priority to the independence and freedom of Iran.

Khomeini rejected what he called 'nation-worshipping' (*melli gara'i*), and he also rejected the prefix of 'democratic' for the Islamic Republic on the ground that Islamic democracy was superior to all other democracies in the world. He in fact rejected the post-Westphalian Western concept of the international system because the nation-state system was, he thought, the creature of weak human minds. His world view called for making the world safe for Islam.

In Khomeini's theory of international relations, all other world views, especially the capitalist and socialist ones, were defunct. For example, when writing to the Soviet leader Mikhail Gorbachev, he castigated the bankrupt 'ideological vacuum' of the East and the West, advocated Islamic values and suggested that Gorbachev study Muslim philosophers and religious thinkers. He even listed them by name. He also pressed his outlook on Iran's neighbours, telling them to establish governments similar to Iran's, to cut their 'subservient ties' with the superpowers and to seek safety under the Iranian security umbrella (*chattr-e amniyat*).

But in practice, Khomeini's concept of independence was tailored to the interests of the Islamic-Iranian state (*ummul qara*). The most telling example of this was Iran's arms purchases from the 'Great Satan', America, during the war with Iraq. Another notable example was his acceptance of the United Nations resolution for a ceasefire with Iraq in 1988. This was in essence to preserve Iran's independence when the tide of war was turning against it. He said that what he did was 'in the interest of the survival (*baqa*) of the revolution', even though it was like drinking poison.

President Hashemi Rafsanjani's concept of independence in effect downplayed Khomeini's transnational Islamic world view and defined it in terms of Iran's control of its decision-making process. For example, he said during his landmark visit to the Soviet Union in 1989 that 'the important development in our country after the revolution is that the people and the authorities decide for themselves without *allowing* the intervention of any foreign elements' (italic added). In retrospect, he shared Khomeini's view, particularly about Iran's need for foreign aid, which the latter had characterized as an 'undisputed fact' in his will and testament.

In practice, Rafsanjani, as president for two terms, from 1989 to 1997, undertook an unprecedented expansion of Iran's foreign relations. He believed that Iran's sovereign independence required its integration into the world community, particularly the world economy. This stance was an important acknowledgement of the limits of Iran's independence. Early in the revolution, Khomeini had said that 'we must isolate ourselves in order to achieve independence' (*bayad monzavi shavim ta mostaqel shavim*), although subsequently he castigated the isolationists, telling them that isolation would mean 'defeat' and 'annihilation'. In practice Khomeini changed his own line.

President Muhammad Khatami combined the conception of independence with 'Islamic democracy', on the fundamental premise that Islam and democracy are compatible. This notion clearly differentiated it from the Western notion of secular and liberal democracy. It also brought down to earth the notion of an Islamic world order. In Khatami's perspective, Iran's independence and freedom were defined in terms of Iran as a nation-state. The most succinct statement of his view of democracy was published in the United Nations Human Development Report 2002: *Deepening Democracy in a Fragmented World*. To summarize, he accepts the reality of democracy, which has evolved over the past century as a value; he rejects any one form of democracy as 'the one and final version' and advocates the formulation of democracy 'in the context of spirituality and morality'. I shall return to this subject below.

In practice, Khatami's conception of independence enjoyed a significant degree of success as a result of Iran's generally conciliatory and proactive foreign policy. The offer to exchange scholars, athletes and others between America and Iran at the outset of his presidency; the restoration of relations with European powers; negotiations with Britain, France and Germany over nuclear energy issues; cooperation with the International Atomic Energy Authority; *rapprochement* with the Persian Gulf states, especially Saudi Arabia; moral and financial support of the nascent Karzai government of Afghanistan; maintenance of constructive relations with China and Russia; efforts to integrate Iran into the international community; and other positive measures redounded to Iran's national interest. But tensions with the United States in 2005 and more recently have been at a record high.

The United States accuses Iran of having nuclear weapons ambitions, of supporting terrorist activities (particularly in view of Iran's ties to Hizbullah in Lebanon and Hamas in Palestine), of working towards the destruction of Israel and obstructing the peace process between Israelis and Palestinians, and supplying lethal arms to Iraqi Shia militas. Iran, on the other hand, accuses the United States of wanting regime change in Iran, of continuing its freeze on Iranian assets, of exerting economic sanctions and diplomatic pressures against it, of threatening military action and of supporting Israeli threats of air strikes against its nuclear facilities. The American about-face in talking to Iran directly in regard to the stabilization of Iraq in May and again in July 2007, however, was combined with an unprecedented increase of American forces in the Persian Gulf aimed at countering the growing influence of Iran in the Middle East.

Contrary to the assumption that Khomeini forbade talking to America, he left the door of negotiations with Washington ajar, suggesting Iran's willingness to resume relations with the United States 'if America behaves itself' (*agar adam beshavad*), that is, if America refrains from dominating Iran. But if Iran and the United States each wait for the other to behave itself, relations between the two countries will remain frozen, as they have been between Cuba and the United States.

As a first step towards a détente, both sides need to stop demonizing each other. Instead they should empathize with each other. Mutual satanization clouds their images of each other and undermines their ability to see clearly that there are areas of genuine common interest between them, particularly in regard to stabilization in Afghanistan and Iraq. They also have common interest in combatting the threat of international terror led by al-Qaida terrorists.

The Long View

I have looked backward, to see if I can look further forward. To summarize, and to try to take a long view of the principles of independence, freedom and the Islamic Republic, let us take independence first. Three points need to be made. First, the record shows beyond doubt that in the past 200 years, Iranian policy-makers have seldom been so much in control of their decision-making process as they have been since the revolution.

Second, there is little doubt that Iranian foreign policy-makers have carefully taken into account their geopolitical environment at both the regional and global levels and have since 1979 been able to defend Iran's national security interests in war and peace. Khomeini's acceptance of the ceasefire with Iraq in 1988 had as much to do with the protection of Iran's territorial integrity as it did, in his words, with 'the survival of the revolution'. Whether during the eight years of defensive war against Iraq or in the face of American and Israeli military threats, national security interests have been given the highest priority, even at the expense of domestic freedoms. The same is the case with some other nations, weak or strong. In the United States, for example, many Americans have become concerned that the Bush administration's overwhelming emphasis on national security and military power since the terrorist attacks on New York and Washington on 11 September 2001 is threatening their civil liberties.

Third, Iranian foreign policy-makers are well aware of the limits of Iran's independence. They have effectively left behind the early isolationist tendencies. They rationalize their current pragmatic foreign policy orientation in terms of Khomeini's pronouncements. Khomeini admonished Islamic zealots in the earliest phase of the revolution, when they objected to his decisions to establish relations with Turkey and Germany. He said that establishing relations with other countries is compatible not only with the Islamic prophetic tradition but also with Iranian national interests. Failure to establish relations, he warned sternly, would mean 'defeat and annihilation' for Iran.

This awareness of the limits of Iranian power to be absolutely independent must be deepened, because the evolution of the objective world is fast leaving behind the complete sovereign independence of nations. The quest for an independent foreign policy in today's dot.com world in the end must continue to cope with degrees of dependence. Today there is immense demand for scientific knowledge and technical expertise. How independent are energy-dependent powerful industrial democracies? How independent are capital- and know-how-starved less-developed countries? The West took some 400 years of evolution to be where it is today, but it will make the equivalent of 20,000 years of progress in science and technology in only one century. Such a pace of change is bound to produce a world of such interdependence that to underestimate its impact on life could amount to committing national suicide.

In view of the staggering pace of evolution of the objective world, the younger generation of Iranians reject and select different strands of their Persian–Islamic tradition of independence. They reject independence if it means territorial expansion, whether justified in the name of Mazdaism or Islamism. They also reject the idea that Iran can be an island sufficient unto itself. But they take pride in their country's glorious past with the same fervour as did Ferdowsi when he sang for 30 years of the love of pre-Islamic Iran. This same profound and patriotic sentiment prompted the moderate and softly-spoken Khatami to warn America and Israel of Iran's retaliatory 'fire of hell' response to any attack on Iran. Recent polls are said to show that 92 per cent of Iranians profess to be 'very proud' of their nationality compared with 72 per cent of Americans.

At the same time, Iranian political culture shows a 'freedom deficit' that lies at the heart of arbitrary laws and injustice. In turn the breakdown of the rule of law and politicized judiciary will ultimately undercut Iran's ability to maintain its independence in world politics. The first Iranian constitution and the present one postulate that freedom and independence are inseparable. But in reality, freedom has not fared well. This striking phenomenon cannot easily be explained, although one might conjecture that Iran's geo-strategic environment and its oil and gas resources have invited foreign invasion, occupation and intervention. As a result, protecting Iran's independence and security has often taken priority over the promotion of freedom. Be that as it may, the historical record and objective accounts demonstrate that the revolution's promise of freedom is yet to be realized.

Two factors in particular necessitate the fulfilment of the promise of reforms. First, the demand for freedom in Iran is growing and unstoppable, despite diehard repression in the name of Islam. Ironically, the processes of Islamization have fuelled the notion of secularization, just as the shah's forcible modernization aided the onset of Islamization. Many Iranians have been inoculated against Islamic extremism. As already noted, the quest for democratic freedom is a century old, and it strikes deep roots in Iran's history and culture. But the Iranian revolution has intensified this quest in an unprecedented way, for a variety of reasons. I suggest that the real engine of the demand for freedom, particularly among the 70 per cent of the population that is under the age of 30, is primarily driven by what I call 'episystemic revolution'. It means that there has been an unprecedented increase in the number of educated people and the people's discourse about religion, society, culture and politics has reached a new height.

Second, the Iranian people, especially younger women and men, are well aware of the spread of democracy worldwide. In the 1997 presidential elections millions of voters demanded social, economic and political change and the integration of Iran into the international community. This show of people's political awakening was unprecedented in the Iranian political history in part because of the march of democracy in the world. Whereas during the era of the Constitutional Revolution, only a handful of countries were democratic, today about half of the world's countries are governed by some form of democracy. That is twice the number of countries as when the Islamic revolution erupted.

Also in contrast to the era of the Constitutional Revolution the Iranians today understand the meaning of freedom quite differently. During the Constitutional Revolution, many Iranians mistook freedom for license. They looted (*chapavol*) and killed revengefully. They now take freedom to mean personal responsibility, home and communication privacy, civil society, the rule of law, government accountability, freedom of religion, press and assembly, free and fair elections, well-informed Majlis representatives, and an independent judiciary. Yet they continue to face serious political abuse of human rights. I believe that if the regime observes in practice the Universal Declaration of Human Rights and related conventions it would go a long way towards earning significant international respect for Iran's sense of independence and the quest for freedom.

But the regime's contrary behaviour has increased people's apathy, particularly after their large participation in the 1997 and 2001 elections in part because of the perceived failures of the Khatami presidency to lighten the burdens of unemployment and inflation. Ironically that apathy worked to the benefit of Mahmood Ahmadinejad in the presidential elections of 2005. He promised the people a better economic life, but his failure to deliver after two years in power has increased people's frustration, especially because the economic failures are compounded by increased political repression.

Third, and finally, the principle of the 'Islamic Republic' remains to be considered. The 'freedom deficit' has increased scepticism about the role of Islam in politics. The tendency to entertain the idea of the separation of religion and politics is growing. For example, some young people seem reluctant to take seriously Ayatollah Hashemi Rafsanjani's propositions articulated on 30 January 2005 that Khomeini's motto of 'independence, freedom and the Islamic Republic' came from the people, that God does not appoint the religious guardians (*faqih*), and that the people do not need his permission to elect their representatives. Their right to vote, said Rafsanjani, is based on custom (*urf*).

Popular distrust of government applies also to President Khatami's farewell address of 10 February 2005 in which he rejected the idea of the separation of religion and state and proposed that 'our country is moving towards democratic Islam, freedom and development' based on his version of 'Islamic democracy'. Some believe that many people, especially the younger generation, are estranged from the concept of Islamic democracy because of the failure of Khatami's social and political reforms. He himself once again frankly admitted his failures and asked for the forgiveness of Allah and the people for his 'failures'.

Given the persistent legacies of Iran's 'freedom deficit', the critics of Khatami's policies are often unfair. They must recognize in fairness the demonstrable fact that no single political leader in Iran's political history over the past two centuries has contributed as much to the popularization of the discourse on democracy as Khatami. It is also worth noting by way of comparison that Western conceptions of democracy developed over centuries of religious, social and political reforms before the Enlightenment, which in part reflected a revolutionary shift of conception from an essentially God-centred to a Man-centred universe. This change celebrates human reason and protects human faith without state interference in the exercise of revelation and reason. Every nation, including Iran, has to work out for itself the relationship between faith and reason, but in today's impatient and fast-paced world humanity cannot take centuries to make change. Liberty is a universal value today, and the people across the world demand it increasingly.

In addressing President Khatami at the United Nations in 2000, I concluded my remarks by saying that I believe there can be no durable political order without equitable justice under the law and no justice without liberty.

I would like to emphasize this conviction, particularly now because of the grievous setbacks that freedom has suffered since 2005.

2

Foreign Policy Theories: Implications for the Foreign Policy Analysis of Iran

Ali Akbar Rezaei

Introduction

The political debate since the 1950s over how Iran's foreign policy should be explained, and how predictable the behaviour of this country is, accelerated from the early days of the revolution and continues vigorously today. Dramatic changes in Iran's foreign policy after the revolution in 1979 challenged the expectations of it, regionally and internationally, to the extent that 'calculations about the Islamic republic have been on the domestic and foreign-policy agendas of most regional actors and key international players'.[1] This debate has been more taxing because Iran's external environment has in turn brought reciprocal challenges to its foreign policy.

America's inclusion of the Islamic Republic in the 'axis of evil' and its raising of the notion of regime change, along with its removal of the Taliban in Afghanistan and the occupation of Iraq, has engendered the foreign policy dilemma of Iran. On the one hand, we can expect a status quo policy from Iran. On the other, we can see Iran as an ambitious power that is looking for major regional and international changes to revive the so-called 'Persian Empire'.

In this chapter I want to put forward a way of analyzing Iran's foreign policy by emphasizing the role of national identity and bureaucratic culture.

Theoretical Approach

Given that all observations are selective and theory-laden, one can only explain Iranian foreign policy by the theoretical approach of international relations (IR). Scholarly debates about theory in IR since its inception after the Second World War have generally been concerned with providing a reliable instrument for watching international events, including those in the Middle East and Iran's behaviour. Improvements in this interdiscipline have taken place through epistemological, ontological and methodological debates. In one debate, traditionalism was methodologically challenged by behaviouralism, but behaviouralism failed to answer many questions and was replaced by post-behaviouralism. The revival of realism by neo-realists led to a new debate with neoliberalism in IR. In the ongoing debate between rationalists, including both neoliberals and neo-realists, and constructivists, different perspectives of ontology and epistemology are discussed. 'Neorealists see the structure of the international system as a distribution of material capabilities . . . Neoliberals see it as capabilities plus institutions . . . and constructivists see it as a distribution of ideas.'[2]

In fact, the debate is rooted in the philosophy of science. This field has been polarized epistemologically between a majority who view science as a privileged discourse through which we can gain a progressively truer understanding of the world and a large minority who do not recognize a privileged status for science in explaining the world 'out there'.[3] Ontologically, this debate has been conducted between those who believe in a world 'out there' and those who believe in a constructed world or the world of ideas.

For the most part, these epistemological and ontological debates are overlapping. For example, Carl Popper, as a scientific realist, cannot suggest that science is 'problem-solving' and 'refutable' unless he assumes a world 'out there' and the responsibility of science to 'explain' that world.[4] Otherwise, one might only be able to 'understand' the world through the relative assumptions of the latter parts of debates.[5] As a case in point, Thomas Kuhn, as a social constructivist, claims that scientific revolution involves paradigm shifts so deep and far-reaching that the meaning of terms from one paradigm to the next may be incommensurable.[6] But he is not able to say this without assuming a world of ideas and relativism, which 'is a form of epistemological antirealism, denying that what is judged, as something independent of the judgment, determines the validity of the judgment'.[7]

Entering these debates in IR, constructivists, on the one hand, believe in 'ideas all the way down'. International politics, in their view, is in the process of being made all the time. They believe in 'understanding' states' actions (*not* behaviour) because they are intentional. On the other hand, rationalists assume the interest and power of states to be 'exogenously given' variables. That is why they claim to 'explain' states' behaviour and are known as rationalists. They include ideational variables in their theories though juxtaposing them to material variables and assuming causal relations between them, i.e. a state's identity causes its national interests. But these relations in constructivist theories are 'constitutive', i.e. national interests are constituted by national identity.

Some scholars consciously attempt to use social theories in order to include both material and ideational variables in IR theory. Barry Buzan, basing his theories on the English school of IR, tries to understand how polarity at the international level and the identity of states play into each other by locating polarity within a social context.[8] He takes

> as given that there is a society of states which has its own rules, norms and institutions. The character of this society is itself open to change as some institutions die out (e.g. colonialism), others rise to prominence (e.g. nationalism during the nineteenth century, the market and multilateralism during the nineteenth and twentieth centuries) and yet others remain in place but get reinterpreted in ways that alter the practices that they legitimate (e.g. sovereignty and non-intervention, war and balance of power during the second half of the twentieth century). The society of states is the container within which the distribution of capabilities and the logic of power politics operate. Sometimes the social structure will line up with, and reinforce, the logic of power politics . . . Sometimes the social structure will undercut the logic of power politics.[9]

Alexander Wendt, in his 'via media' theory, has proposed causal and constitutive relations between material and ideational variables in order to take advantage of both realism and constructivism. He

> assume[s] that the process of identity- and interest-formation have created a world in which states do not recognize rights to territory or existence – war of all against all. In this world, anarchy has a 'realist' meaning for state action: be insecure and concerned with relative power. Anarchy has this meaning only in virtue of collective, insecurity-producing practices, but if those practices are relatively stable, they do constitute a system that may resist change. The fact that worlds of power politics are socially constructed, in other words, does not guarantee they are malleable.[10]

In understanding Wendt's theory, one should keep in mind that he believes in 'no fundamental epistemological difference between Explanation and Understanding'.[11] In fact, this controversial claim is aimed at reconciling the proponents of rationalism and constructivism in IR through the via media solution.

International Relations and Foreign Policy Analysis

Although the study of foreign policy was included in IR at its beginning, it began to be a new subfield as a result of the seminal work of Richard Snyder, H.W. Bruck and Burton Sapin, the founding fathers of foreign policy analysis (FPA), more than 40 years ago.[12] Despite receiving some very important contributions from IR, such as idealism and realism indications, FPA still defies its grand theories. The lack of an appropriate approach and, in consequence, contradictions in existing theories, among other things, gave rise to this problem. Therefore, analysts still cannot claim to understand what exactly is going on in the 'black box' of states' foreign policies.

In brief, 'intersubjective' / 'interobjective' 'explanation' of agent and structure in international relations is reduced to explaining an actor's behaviour or action in FPA. By way of example, Wendt's proposition that 'anarchy is what states make of it'[13] in IR theory has been reduced in FPA to, as Steven Smith says, 'foreign policy is what states make of it'.[14] But contrary to Wendt, Smith fails to introduce a foreign policy theory. This is true as well of most other theoretical studies of FPA. As was clearly mentioned a long time ago by Rosenau, FPA is still devoid of general theory – there is no doubt.[15] In view of this, Valerie Hudson suggests a more reductionist approach in studying foreign policy, one that is 'multifactoral', 'multilevel', 'multi-interdisciplinary', 'integrative', 'agent oriented' and 'actor specific', in order to overcome the theoretical shortcomings.[16]

Although one should not expect a mature theoretical explanation of foreign policy that is acceptable to a majority of experts in this field – let alone Iran's foreign policy, which is a more challenging case study – there is no other option than to rely on existing achievements while calling for more research in this field. It follows that Iran's foreign policy must be examined through the existing theoretical frameworks. Examining the case of Iran is as useful as discussing other countries of the same importance and complexity in helping to improve foreign policy analysis. On the one hand, Iran's foreign policy-makers have been influenced by the theoretical debates outlined above; on the other hand, its foreign policy has challenged theoretical achievements in FPA. Looking for Iran in the index of most of the scholarly books in this field shows many examples of these reciprocal influences.

What to Study in Iran's Foreign Policy

Iran's foreign policy raises many unanswered questions. What should one know about Iran's foreign policy? How does Iran define its interests and choose to pursue them? Is this a matter to be explained or to be understood? Is its foreign policy based on words or deeds, behaviour or action? Should the analyst attempt to find out the causes of Iran's policies or the reasons for them? Are the causes or the effects of Iranian foreign policy to be addressed? Are its variables subjective or objective? Are they material or ideational? What is the role of culture in that policy, and is it prior to its rationale? Is it scientific at all to talk about Iran's 'foreign policy'? Can we have a theory or model of it at all?

To answer these questions, one should consider the implications of the FPA debates for the analysis of Iran's foreign policy. Among those debates, three are particularly appropriate: international relations versus regional studies, actor-general studies versus actor-specific studies and rationalism versus constructivism.

IR versus Regional Studies

The IR mainstream believes that common rules apply to all states but specialists on developing states tend to differentiate the behaviour of these states from others. Thus the foreign policy analysis of Middle Eastern states has been polarized between generalists, who insist that universal rules apply to all regions and areas, and specialists, who defend the cultural uniqueness and consequent political exceptionalism of the Middle East.[17] There are, for example, some regional specialists who believe that the foreign policy of a Middle Eastern state is shaped by the way its leaders deal with the often conflicting pressures emanating from three conceptually distinct environments, at the domestic, regional and international levels.[18] In more detail, Gerd Nonneman believes that the Middle Eastern states' foreign policies 'have in varying ways been determined by the needs of the regimes at home, the changing availability of resources, and [the] international strategic and economic framework within which these countries have played a subordinate but not necessarily powerless role'.[19]

Despite including many variables, these explanations are not regional theories. They have, at best, applied realism to the Middle Eastern states' foreign policies. A regional theory should be different, at least by having regional assumptions.

I shall mention two regional theories by way of example. First, Dale Eickelman and James Piscatori in their book *Muslim Politics* imply that there are both constructivist and rationalist ingredients in Islamic states' policies. They believe that Islam constitutes the language of politics in the Muslim world, although through multiple interpretations. 'Islamic vocabulary contains words of undoubted political resonance, and a review of their historical development helps to explain their durable attraction.'[20] Despite the importance of the 'language of politics', they take into account the 'politics of language' in the Islamic world. As such, in an Islamic state 'values and interests are not radically divorced from each other, and, of course, values can be interests and interests can be valued'.[21]

Based on this theoretical approach, Eickelman and Piscatori try to explain Islamic states' behaviour through a mixed theoretical framework by giving many good examples. Their approach addresses pan-Islamism, as the main foreign policy issue in Islamic states. 'Just as the emergence of a universal Islamic state is not on the horizon, neither are forms of pan-Islamic activity missing from the political geography of Muslims.'[22] In elaboration, they argue that in the case of Islam, vertical transnationalism is lacking but that there are ways in which a horizontal transnationalism may be said to have political significance.[23] By 'vertical transnationalism', they mean a universal Islamic state. However, by 'horizontal transnationalism' they refer to the three issues of the 'call' to Islam, concern over the plight of Muslim minorities and concern over a number of Muslim issues such as Palestine, Afghanistan and Bosnia.[24]

Influenced by the current debate in IR, the core concept of their theoretical framework is the notion of Muslim 'agency', in the sense that the sociologist Anthony Giddens uses the term: an individual's or group's capability to intervene, or to refrain from intervening, in a series of events so as to influence its course. Therefore, they conclude,

'Muslims increasingly perceive that Islam offers them agency, but not in the sense of a monolithic force'.[25]

In the second regional theory, Fred Halliday proposes 'historical sociology' as a way to explain Middle Eastern states' foreign policies. This approach, like realism, 'gives prominence to the "state", even while its conception of the state is a very different one. Equally it shares common ground with foreign policy analysis in looking at domestic context, but retains a concept of the states as a distinct institutional category, not the sum of myriad decisions.'[26] In it, foreign policy is 'a product not just of personal and bureaucratic process within the state but of interests, and clashes, of state and class alike. Ideology and norms are central, not as the constitutive domain of politics, but rather as part of the process of legitimation and coercion.'[27] In other words, domestic legitimation can be viewed as the main function of foreign policy in the Middle East, but ideology is taken as the driving force of foreign policy.

Halliday suggests the via media theory in order to use both ideology and legitimation. The ideology of the state is important from his point of view: it is not to be taken only at face value; it also provides legitimacy. However, he does not deny that ideational variables, such as ideology, can make a difference in the foreign policy of Middle Eastern countries. But even so, Halliday, like Piscatori and Eickelman, tries to include both ideational and material variables in his approach. As he says, 'Ideology is *a* factor in foreign policy, but as an *instrument* of states, as much as it is an independent limit on what the state does.'[28] The problem with this approach is that the 'limit' is yet to be clarified.

Actor-general Theories versus Actor-specific Theories

Foreign policy analysis is also divided between those who are looking for actor-general theories by referring to foreign policy outcomes and those who emphasize actor-specific theories, working mainly on foreign policy decision-making processes. Grand theories such as game theory or rational choice modelling are used as actor-general theories. These theories mostly tend to explain and predict through quantifiable variables the propensity of states to go to war. In actor-specific theories, unquantifiable variables such as culture, small-group dynamics and bureaucratic politics are examined.

The end of the Cold War brought a renewed interest in actor-specific theory. Actor-general theory was more practical for scholars to use during the Cold War because the Soviet system was fairly opaque.[29] But the dominant actor-general theories had failed to predict and justify the collapse of the Soviet Union and were seriously challenged by actor-specific theories.

Recent Middle Eastern studies, including those of Iran's foreign policy, have shown an increasing interest in applying actor-specific theories. Important issues such as the political psychology of leaders, bureaucratic politics and national identity are discussed in this body of research.[30]

Yet again the problem is about whether one should accept reductionism in science in order to answer all questions. In Popper's words, actor-specific theories cannot be scientific because they cannot be 'refutable'. 'If a theory is incompatible with possible empirical observations it is scientific; conversely, a theory which is compatible with all such observations, either because, as in the case of Marxism, it has been modified solely to accommodate such observations, or because, as in the case of psychoanalytic theories, it is consistent with all possible observations, is unscientific.'[31]

Rationalism versus Constructivism

The current debate in IR between rationalists and constructivists has influenced foreign policy analysis. Realists and neorealists are rationalist because they assume that the interests of states are 'exogenously given'. In Wendtian constructivism, interests are also constituted by identity. But one may find that neither theory is appropriate to FPA. Moreover, there are some among the spectrum of constructivists who believe that the via media theory of Wendt is not a real constructivist theory. Smith believes that Wendt 'ends up painting a world that seems very similar to that painted by rationalists'.[32]

In that sense, rationalism is applicable only to world politics and FPA is associated with constructivism. For example, Smith proposes an FPA theory through constructivism and assumes that 'actors, whoever they are, are governed by language, rules, and choices'.[33] He believes that it is precisely this form of social constructivism that offers a role for foreign policy rather than treating states as 'a pre-social given' that forms its identity only through interactions with other states.

Scholars such as Smith call themselves 'rule-oriented constructivists'. 'Seeing the social world the way a rule-oriented constructivist [does] involves seeing the world as inextricably social and material, that is, seeing people in their world as makers of their world, and seeing the world as a never-ending construction project.'[34] This approach is rooted in influential social theories in which 'behaviour' is distinguished from 'action' as intentional and normatively guided behaviour, which Habermas calls rule-governed behaviour.[35] Actions in this approach are coordinated primarily by communicatively mediated norms and values in a social context confined and constructed by language or what Wittgenstein called 'language games'.

In a compelling analysis of American foreign policy by Peter Howard, this version of constructivism is applied to explain different US policies towards North Korea and Iraq. Although the United States identified both countries as members of the 'axis of evil', it invaded Iraq but chose to negotiate with North Korea. Howard argues that

> a language-based constructivist approach can explain these differences
> in U.S. foreign policy . . . By examining the U.S. entanglement
> in intersected language games – the implementation of the 1994
> Agreed Framework with North Korea and the enforcement of
> the United Nations Resolutions in Iraq – it becomes possible
> to show how the United States could construct North Korea's
> nuclear program as a manageable threat that could be dealt with
> diplomatically.[36]

In view of this example, one can apply different language games to contradictory Iranian foreign policies for different issues and areas. For instance, Iran has good relations with Syria, an Arab state with a Baath government, but it has fought with Iraq.

Although this approach challenges realism and proposes a replacement, it does not, as Smith accepts, offer a theory about foreign policy.[37] It is, at best, a framework focusing on words and rules. There are 'constructivists' who are seen as understanders, not explainers. And as one of the aims of science is prediction, the constructivist approach fails, and even ignores that fact.

Despite these deep theoretical researches, one can expect at most only an integration of the achievements of the different debates influencing the study of Iran's foreign policy. As a result of those debates, analyses of Iranian foreign policy tend to be more regional, actor-specific and social-based. This has been the principal nature of analyses since the revolution. But the more recent literature shows much interest in working on issues concerning the implications of culture and identity for Iranian foreign policy.

An Overview of the Foreign Policy Analysis of Iran

The study of Iran's foreign policy began some 50 years ago with classical single-country studies, mainly with a historical approach, of Iran's foreign relations. Students owe their knowledge in this respect to R.K. Ramazani, who has reviewed in one of his seminal works the foreign policy of Iran from 1500 to 1900.[38] His work has been followed by studies by Chubin and Zabih[39] and others. These studies, as well as more recent ones in the field, benefit from at least a tacit theoretical framework. Here I examine these theoretical approaches and their gradual improvements.

The Geopolitical Approach

A geopolitical approach posits that historical determinism and geopolitics are the main driving forces behind foreign policy. Accordingly, the foreign policy and national security of Iran are required to have a meaningful internal logic, in tune with global trends, in order for the country to end its security isolation.[40] But this approach is not able to explain, for example, Iran's confrontational policy in the 1980s that left it with only one major ally in the Middle East, which was Syria.[41]

Three geopolitical determinants help to provide a deeper explanation of Iran's predicament. First, Iran has a strong sense of identity, a notable culture and an ancient civilization from which it takes inspiration.[42] Second, Iran's interest in the affairs of oppressed nations worldwide is based on its civilization, which goes back to the pre-Islamic period.[43] Third, Iran is the only Shia Muslim state in the world, and this has heightened both its sense of uniqueness and its sense of isolation.[44]

These historical 'facts' explain, individually and collectively, Iran's behaviour to a large extent. Thus its egalitarian foreign policy can be explained in the light of its civilizational background and its pragmatism can be understood as a consequence of its experience of long-term governance. But a geopolitical approach is limited by the lack of definition in these historical 'facts', many of which are more recent than is usually imagined.[45] Therefore, compared to the impact of, for example, Shiism on Iran's foreign policy, one may find facts about the early Iran more reliable.

However, the problem with ancient historical 'facts' is a lack of reliable information. The ancient history of Iran, for example, was written by a few people. Iran's achievements, whether gleaned through excavation or from others' histories, also remain an 'interpretative exercise'.[46] Given the different motivations and perceptions of scholars, they may overstate or highlight some of the historical facts. Therefore, as Halliday observes, 'the most important question left open . . . is not "whether" history but "which" history'.[47]

The geopolitical approach is also qualified by another development in social science. The displacement of 'traditions' in societies, as elaborated by modernization theories, has challenged the idea that they are a 'given' in Iran and other nations.[48] As historical facts are recognizable through traditions, the question of whether 'culture matters'[49] in societies is important to students of this field. This question has yet to be answered convincingly. But 'cultural studies' are present in today's social sciences, and the conceptual challenges they pose cannot be ignored.

Realism

Although sharing its theoretical assumptions, realism is an alternative to the geopolitical approach. It is a modified version of classical realism and incorporates more recent versions such as neorealism and aggressive realism in IR. This theory is intended to explain international politics, but it is also used sometimes in academic studies to explain the foreign policies of Iran and other Middle Eastern countries. This approach assumes that the actors in the international arena are 'rational'. Ehteshami, for example, believes that revolutionary Iran has always been a 'rational actor' in classic realist terms.[50] He observes that Iran's rationality has much to do with calculations about its standing in a changing regional and international environment. But he does not make clear whether there are criteria for rationalism or whether whatever Iran does is 'rational'.

To explain irregularities in Iran's foreign policy, some scholars assume its gradual tendency towards rationalism. That policy, it is argued, has become 'increasingly prudent'[51] since the revolution, as shown by a gradual maturation and reassertion of national interest and rationality. Putting Iran in the category of a developing Middle Eastern state with a revolutionary background, realists can assume this improvement in its behaviour. But this approach fails to explain what Ramazani has observed of the nature of revolutionary Iran's foreign policy: it is neither 'linear, nor dialectical, but kaleidoscopic'. The 'important cautionary point is that the fluidity of Iranian revolutionary politics is such that today's idealists may be tomorrow's realists and vice versa, and [an] idealist on one set of issues may be [a] realist on another'.[52] The observation of this fluid nature of Iranian politics is an important step towards developing conceptual frameworks that explain the apparently conflicting elements of Iran's foreign policy.

Decision-making in Iranian Foreign Policy

Analysing the decision-making process and its elements has always been a principal focus of many FPA theories. Some analysts try to account for Iran's contradictory foreign policy by pointing to the complexity and apparent chaos of the Iranian policy-making system. They believe that 'the large number of institutional and non institutional actors, family ties, personal relationships, overlapping institutional authority, and [the] mixture of religion and politics all contrive to make it difficult to identify who has a say on what issue. Often many voices are heard and similar issues often involve different actors within the system.'[53] Even though, they recognize, the important players act with the oversight of the senior leadership and with an emphasis on consensus, and so 'the result is often a constant back-and-forth process'.[54] Consequently, 'the direction of Iran's foreign policy is hardly consistent: at times, the revolutionary imperative dominates; at other times, concern over ethnic fragmentation or economic relations predominate.'[55]

In view of these characteristics of Iran's decision-making, one might not have expected significant changes in the Islamic Republic's foreign policy during the reform period. But, as Chubin says, President Khatami changed Iran's policy: it normalized relations with its neighbours and Europe, which had been politically contentious.[56] But bearing in mind that these changes began even before Khatami, in Hashemi's tenure, it may contradict the perception of Iran's foreign policy as an intersubjective variable that decision-making theory fails to address.

Pragmatism

Some research has used pragmatism to explain the contradictory elements of realism and idealism in Iran's foreign policy. Theoretically, as long as realism and idealism are its two main approaches, a state's foreign policy must be either entirely ethical or unethical. But theoretical states do not exist in the real world. The tension between realism and idealism leads to pragmatism, which provides a middle path to explain foreign policies. It breaks down the realist–idealist dichotomy and emphasizes the necessity for states to respond to the realities of world politics.

As for Iran, Ramazani suggests that 'the balance of ideology and pragmatism in the making of [its] foreign policy decisions has been one of the most persistent, intricate and difficult issues in all Iranian history, from the sixth century BC, when the Iranian state was born, to the present time'.[57] Although he uses the term 'pragmatism' instead of rationalism, their meanings are roughly equivalent.

The perennial question must be faced about how to explain the mechanism for providing this balance and for maintaining and applying the criteria for pragmatism. It is observed that pragmatism works from the assumption that ethics must be conceived democratically.[58] In the case of Iran, pragmatism is effected by a cultural and procedural emphasis on consensus, and 'although debates in Iran are often fierce, major decisions seldom go forward without at least a tacit consensus among the elites'.[59]

But the pragmatic approach may end up justifying all decisions as pragmatic. Pragmatism is too underspecified to be able to introduce falsifiable hypotheses. As such, any foreign policy behaviour of Iran can be given as evidence of pragmatism. The historical as well as the contemporary behaviour of Iran provides many examples, such as its relations with the Unites States or even Israel. Thus even the most ideological policies can be explained as pragmatic, as can the most rational ones.

This problem is due in part to the 'domestically given' source of foreign policy. Clearly, the perception of ideology and pragmatism may vary from the national to the international level. And so, no matter how pragmatic it is, 'a pragmatic Iran will still be perceived and treated as revolutionary'.[60] This problem is highlighted by recent developments in IR theories using social science assumptions. Given the social context in which material variables such as the power and interests of different nations are defined, the criteria of pragmatism cannot be the same at the national and international levels.

National Identity and Iran's Foreign Policy
As mentioned earlier, constructivism helps us, epistemologically and ontologically, to understand more about foreign policy by examining

the role of ideational variables such as culture and identity. It assumes that 'culture informs and in many ways determines the priorities a given state affords itself when defining its foreign policy objectives'[61] through national identity.

In rationalist theories, material and ideational factors together create an 'exogenously given' national interest. But in constructivism, the state's interests are constituted by national identity, and national identity is constituted by either internal or external variables. Because in FPA the unit of behaviour is the independent variable rather than the aggregate behaviour of states, it may be inappropriate to use the systemic level of analysis of constructivism in FPA theorizing.

If the systemic level is used in an analysis of Iran's foreign policy, one may talk only about the relational characteristics of Iran's foreign policy in international politics. Mesbahi has recognized two of them:

> First is the strategic loneliness of Iran in the international system and regional sub-system, and second, the securitization of Iran's identity; the impact of ideology and the perception of others which made the assessment of Iran's intentions, capability, threat, to be largely driven not by Iran's material capability and power projection, but by its intentions, message, identity and ideas.[62]

Then he applies these characteristics to Iran's relations with Russia – Iran is particularly influenced by Russia's relations with the United States – to examine the limit of relations between the two countries. As a constructivist, he applies constitutive relations between Iran's capability and intentions and the world structure.

But in order to understand Iran's foreign policy, one needs to know more about its internal effects on the country's national identity. Here the assumption is that the social structure of international politics is not strong enough to generate significant identities for states.[63] The main source of their national identity in this sense would be at the national, decision-making or leaders' level of analysis. Holsti's 'national role conception' is a classic example of a foreign policy theory that attempts to show the process of national-identity articulation by linking the national role concept to human agency.[64]

Recent research on Iran's foreign policy shows a great interest in using related assumptions so as to explain its policy. Ansari, for example, believes that the national identity of Iran consists more or less of a combination of national, religious and Western cultures.[65] Islamic culture has played a formative role in defining Iranian foreign policy objectives, but the interpretation of Islam as a factor of foreign policy varies. National culture takes Iran to a higher level of power politics in its understanding of international relations through moderation and prudence. As for Western culture, it is striking how much Iran has borrowed from the West, starting with the concepts of the republic and revolution. To explain the process of national identity-formation and change, Ansari points to a dialectical process of development in the Iranian national identity. Through this process, one may see a sequence of contradictions emerging that need resolving, either intellectually, practically or coercively, before the next stage can be reached. For example, the notion of Dialogue among Civilizations raised by president Khatami is seen as the synthesis of this dialectical process in Iran.

Sariolghalam adds epistemological changes to the ideational variables of Iran's foreign policy. He believes that early in the revolution, most people viewed foreigners, foreign governments and external elements as fundamentally shaping Iranian politics. But now the expectations of the state of the average Iranian have changed significantly. Theories of imperialism and conspiracy are eroding in the Iranian political con-sciousness. The policy outcome of these developments is an emphasis on pursuing dialogue and engagement with other nations.[66]

The problem with identity-formation theories has been the way in which material and ideational variables are correlated. They cannot be explained simply by juxtaposing identity and power politics in order to understand the impact of identity on foreign policy. A dialectical solution is a step forward, but it still works in a black box. Ansari proposes many possibilities in an effort to explain the process of development of the Iranian national identity, but these need more elaboration.

Maloney, in her seminal chapter on identity in Iran's foreign policy, tries to overcome this problem by illuminating the institutional durability of national identity and its influence on structuring foreign policy choices.[67] She regards national identity as multi-dimensional, not simply as a series of normative alternatives or an affirmative statement of self. She depicts Iranian national identity as a prism of competing influences, including Persian nationalism, Islamism and revolutionary anti-imperialism. With some good examples, she shows the limitations of these three influences in forming Iran's national identity in different eras.

In a contextual assessment, one may have a better understanding of the constitutive relations between real politics and ideational factors that Maloney has provided in her chapter. In her words, 'one cannot understand the foreign policy of the Islamic Republic without appreciating the political factors and the conditioning forces of its ideology at the same time'.[68]

Although her explanation of Iran's foreign policy is comprehensive, one is not able to predict any specific outcome of Iran's foreign policy through this approach because it fails to suggest an appropriate explanation of material and ideational variables interacting with each other to form the Iranian national identity.

Conclusion

To overcome theoretical shortcomings in the foreign policy analysis of Iran, an eclectic approach combining elements from the various current theoretical debates may be appropriate. And although caution is needed, in order to begin problem-solving one should carry out a continuous assessment of what we know and what we do not know about the foreign policy of Iran in order to give direction to gradual improvements in the field. Despite the need for more research to reduce the contradictions between these approaches, their achievements should not be ignored unless major conceptual advances take place in FPA. As Chernoff says, 'one never rejects a theory, regardless of the falsifiable evidence, unless there is an alternative theory available to take its place'.[69]

There are at least two important implications to the mentioned approaches. First, these approaches read Iran's foreign policy as though they are all based on realism. If, for example, Ramazani suggests the 'tradition of prudence' to explain Iran's foreign policy, Ehteshami assumes Iran to be a 'rational actor' in applying classic realism to its behaviour and Halliday proposes 'nationalism' as the driving force of Iran's foreign policy, Maloney will not be able to explain much of Iran's foreign policy unless she uses the notion of a 'religious rationale' in Iranian national identity-making.

Second, one cannot ignore the fact that ideas make a difference and that the crucial idea of 'agency' must be taken into account. Moreover, ideas create an 'intersubjective' concept that must be addressed in any theoretical framework. Wendtian constructivism and Halliday's sociology of the state are the approaches that try to provide a meaningful theoretical framework to include both realism and idealism at the international and regional level respectively. Ehteshami's modified realism and Ramazani's pragmatism also provide answers to the same questions about Iran's foreign policy.

If I were to propose a model to explain Iran's foreign policy, I would create a hybrid one, from Wendtian constructivism and the English school of international relations. In doing so, I would need to apply their assumptions to the national level. In that sense, obviously, one needs to replace the unit level of analysis with the systemic one.

My assumptions would be as follows: first, international society is not so strong that even the great powers' foreign policies are always generated by variables at the international level. 'It is not coincidental, therefore, that the strongest and most meaningful statements regarding American national identity have come from presidents during wartime.'[70] In those cases, the legitimate power of nationalism is employed to furnish the official interpretation of foreign policy. This observation is applicable to Iran's foreign policy to a large extent.

Second, I assume that the national identity of Iran is the context within which its foreign policy is constituted. The ingredients of national identity are domestic and self-referential, however, it may be influenced, directly and indirectly, by the external environment.

Third, just as Wendt proposes the 'culture of anarchy' as the macro-structure at the international level, we may suggest a different 'bureaucratic culture' as the driving force of foreign policy at state level. Accordingly, the causal effect of bureaucracy and the constitutive effects of bureaucratic culture are the main forces behind Iran's foreign policy.

NOTES

1 Anoushiravan Ehteshami, 'The Foreign Policy of Iran', in Raymond Hinnebusch and Anoushiravan Ehteshami (eds), *The Foreign Policies of Middle East States* (London: Lynne Rienner, 2002), pp. 283–310.

2 Alexander Wendt, *Social Theory of International Politics* (Cambridge: Cambridge University Press, 1999), p. 5.

3 Ibid., p. 38.

4 *Stanford Encyclopedia of Philosophy*, at http://plato.stanford.edu/entries/popper/#Life.

5 For more information on the distinction between understanding and explanation in IR, see Martin Hollis and Steven Smith, *Explaining and Understanding International Relations* (Oxford: Clarendon Press, 1990).

6 Lawrence E. Cahoone, *Cultural Revolutions: Reason versus Culture in Philosophy, Politics, and Jihad* (University Park, PA: Pennsylvania University Press, 2005), p. 148.

7 Ibid., p. 151.

8 Barry Buzan, *The United States and the Great Powers: World Politics in the Twenty-First Century* (Cambridge: Polity Press, 2004), pp. 2–3.

9 Ibid., pp. 3–4.

10 Alexander Wendt, 'Anarchy is What States Make of It: the Social Construction of Power Politics', *International Organization*, vol. 46, 1992, pp. 410–11.

11 Wendt, *Social Theory of International Politics*, p. 85.

12 R.C. Snyder, W. Bruck and B. Sapin (eds), *Foreign Policy Decision-Making: An Approach to the Study of International Politics* (Glencoe, IL: Free Press, 1962).

13 Wendt, 'Anarchy is What States Make of It', pp. 391–425.

14 Steven Smith, 'Foreign Policy is What States Make of It: Social Construction and International Relations Theory', in Vendulka Kubalkova (ed.), *Foreign Policy in a Constructed World* (London: M.E. Sharpe, 2001), pp. 38–55.

15 James Rosenau, 'Pre-Theories and Theories of Foreign Policy', in R.B. Farrell (ed.), *Approaches in Comparative and International Politics* (Evanston: Northwestern University Press, 1966), p. 99.

16 Valerie Hudson, 'Foreign Policy Analysis: Actor-Specific Theory and the Ground of International Relations', *Foreign Policy Analysis*, vol. 1, 2005, pp. 1–30.

17 Raymond Hinnebusch, 'Explaining International Politics in the Middle East: The Struggle of Regional Identity and System Structure', in Gerd Nonneman (ed.), *Analyzing Middle East Foreign Policies and the Relationship with Europe* (London: Routledge, 2005), pp. 243–56.

18 Hinnebusch and Ehteshami (eds), *Foreign Policies of Middle East States*, p. 2.

19 Gerd Nonneman, 'Analyzing the Foreign Policy of the Middle East and North Africa: A Conceptual Framework', in ibid., pp. 6–18.

20 Dale Eickelman and James Piscatori, *Muslim Politics* (Princeton: Princeton University Press, 2004), p. 12.

21 Ibid., p. 59.

22 Ibid., p. 141.

23 Ibid., pp. 141–2.

24 Ibid., pp. 142–6.

25 Ibid., p. 162.

26 Fred Halliday, *The Middle East in International Relations: Power, Politics and Ideology* (Cambridge: Cambridge University Press, 2005), pp. 35–6.

27 Ibid., p. 37.

28 Ibid., p. 66.

29 Hudson, 'Foreign Policy Analysis', pp. 1–30.

30 See Raymond Hinnebusch, 'Explaining International Politics in the Middle East: The Struggle of Regional Identity and System Structure', in Gerd Nonneman (ed.), *Analyzing Middle East Foreign Policies and the Relationship with Europe* (London: Routledge, 2005), pp. 243–56.

31 *Stanford Encyclopedia of Philosophy*, at http://plato.stanford.edu/entries/popper/#Life.

32 Steven Smith, 'Foreign Policy is What States Make of It', pp. 38–55.

33 Idem.

34 Vendulka Kubalkova, 'A Constructivist Primer', in Kubalkova (ed.), *Foreign Policy in a Constructed World*, p. 58.

35 Jurgen Habermas, *On the Pragmatics of Social Interaction: Preliminary Studies in the Theory of Communicative Action*, trans. Barbara Fultner (Cambridge: Polity Press, 2002), pp. 4–6.

36 Peter Howard, 'Why Not Invade North Korea? Threats, Language Games, and U.S. Foreign Policy', *International Studies Quarterly*, vol. 48, 2004, p. 805.

37 Steven Smith, 'Foreign Policy is What States Make of It'.

38 Rouhollah Ramazani, *The Foreign Policy of Iran, 1500–1941: A Developing Nation in World Affairs* (Charlottesville, Virginia: University of Virginia Press, 1966).

39 Shahram Chubin and Sepehr Zabih, *The Foreign Relations of Iran: A Developing State in a Zone of Great Power Conflict* (London: University of California Press, 1974).

40 Mahmood Sariolghalam, 'Justice for All', *The Washington Quarterly*, Summer 2001, pp. 113–26.

41 Rouhollah Ramazani, 'Iran's Foreign Policy: Contending Orientations', in R. Ramazani (ed.), *Iran's Revolution: The Search for Consensus* (Washington, DC: The Middle East Institute, 1990), pp. 48–68.

42 Shahram Chubin, 'Iran's Strategic Predicament', *The Middle East Journal*, vol. 50, 2000, p. 15.

43 Nikki Keddie, *Modern Iran: Roots and Result of the Revolution* (New Haven: Yale University Press, 2003), p. 3.

44 Pollack, *The Persian Puzzle: The Conflict Between Iran and America* (New York: Random House, 2004), pp. 4–5.

45 Keddie, *Modern Iran*, p. 9.

46 Ali Ansari, *A History of Modern Iran since 1921: The Pahlavis and After* (London: Routledge and Curzon, 2004), p. 11.

47 Halliday, *The Middle East in International Relations*, p. 24.

48 Eickelman and Piscatori, *Muslim Politics*, ch. 2.

49 See Lawrence Harrison and Samuel Huntington (eds), *Culture Matters: How Values Shape Human Progress* (New York: Basic Books, 2001).

50 Anoushiravan Ehteshami, 'The Foreign Policy of Iran', in Hinnebusch and Ehteshami (eds), *The Foreign Policies of Middle East States*, pp. 283–310.

51 Daniel Bayman, Shahram Chubin, Anoushiravan Ehteshami and Jerald Green, *Iran's Security Policy in the Post-Revolutionary Era* (Santa Monica, California: Rand, 2001), p. 100.

52 Rouhollah Ramazani, 'Iran's Foreign Policy', in Ramazani (ed.), *Iran's Revolution*, p. 59.

53 Bayman, Chubin, Ehteshami and Green, *Iran's Security Policy in the Post-Revolutionary Era*, pp. 21–2.

54 Ibid., p. 23.

55 Ibid., p. 53.

56 Shahram Chubin, *Whither Iran? Reform, Domestic Politics and National Security* (London: International Institute for Strategic Studies, 2002), p. 17.

57 Rouhollah Ramazani, 'Ideology and Pragmatism in Iran's Foreign Policy', *The Middle East Journal*, vol. 58, Winter 2004, p. 549.

58 M. Cochran, 'A Pragmatic Perspective on Ethical Foreign Policy', in K. Smith and M. Light (eds), *Ethics and Foreign Policy* (Cambridge: Cambridge University Press, 2001), p. 58.

59 Bayman, Chubin, Ehteshami and Green, *Iran's Security Policy in the Post-Revolutionary Era*, p. 22.

60 Mohiaddin Mesbahi, 'Iran and Central Asia: Paradigm and Policy', *Central Asian Survey*, vol. 23, 2004, p. 117.

61 A. Ansari, 'Civilizational Identity and Foreign Policy: the Case of Iran', unpublished article, September 2003.

62 Mesbahi, 'Iran and Central Asia', p. 110.

63 Wendt, *Social Theory of International Politics*, p. 227.

64 See K. Holsti, 'National Role Conception in the Study of Foreign Policy', *International Studies Quarterly*, vol. 14 (Sep., 1970), pp. 233–309.

65 Ansari, 'Civilizational Identity and Foreign Policy'.

66 Sariolghalam, 'Justice for All', pp. 113–25.

67 Suzanne Maloney, 'Identity and Change in Iran's Foreign Policy', in Shibley Telhami and Michael Barnett (eds), *Identity and Foreign Policy in the Middle East* (New York: Cornell University Press, 2002), pp. 88–116.

68 Ibid, pp. 88–116.

69 Fred Chernoff, 'Scientific Realism as a Meta-Theory of International Politics', *International Studies Quarterly*, vol. 46, 2002, p. 205.

70 Paul McCartney, 'American Nationalism and U.S. Foreign Policy from September 11 to the Iraq War', *Political Science Quarterly*, vol. 119, 2004, pp. 407–8.

3

The United States and Iran in Iraq:
Risks and Opportunities

Judith S. Yaphe

What is the perception of Iran as seen from Washington by the United States, the world's self-declared sole superpower? It is encircled by pro-American governments and American forces in Kabul and Baghdad and American forces and assets prepositioned in Central Asia, the Persian Gulf and the Indian Ocean. What is the perception of the United States as seen from Tehran, the home of the Shia Islamic revolution and the occasional pre-eminent power of the Persian Gulf? It is encircled by Muslims. When Americans look across the borders of Iraq and outside the Green Zone in Baghdad, they see Muslims everywhere.

These are dramatic times in the region called the Persian Gulf on its northern shore and the Arabian Gulf on its southern shore. Since 2001, it has seen regime change by violent means in Afghanistan, Iraq, and Lebanon; political succession by natural causes in Saudi Arabia, the United Arab Emirates and Kuwait; national elections in Afghanistan, Iraq, Iran, Palestine, Lebanon, Egypt and Kuwait; and municipal elections in Qatar, Bahrain, Oman and even Saudi Arabia. Iran has held elections for municipal councils, the parliament (Majlis) and the presidency – all won by hard-liners – and it has seen the rise to power of its first elected non-cleric president since the revolution, Mahmoud Ahmadinejad. It is also witnessing the rise to political power of former members of the military and security services who share the experiences and uncompromising world-view of the new president. Iraq held three elections in 2005, its first truly free exercise of political power in at least 50 years, two of them parliamentary elections both of which were won by the country's Shia majority parties.

The opinions expressed here are the author's and do not represent policies of the National Defense University, the Department of Defense or any other US government agency.

What is happening in the region after long years of autocratic rule, suppression of dissent, closed societies and psychological, if not actual, foreign occupation? What do the above events have in common? And what do they mean to the current rivals for hegemony in the Gulf – the United States and Iran? All its countries are talking about democracy and holding elections; all are experiencing what advisers to the Bush administration call the 'springtime of reform'. It is an awakening those advisers also take credit for, believing that regime change in Iraq has given birth to rising demands for political reform, social change and the empowerment of women and of ethnic and sectarian groups.

Iran too takes credit for many of these changes. Its Islamic revolution in 1979 was, after all, the first postmodern revolution in the region, and it introduced theocratic democracy, Islamic governance and sharia-based law. It cannot be easy to see America's military presence and political influence so entrenched in the region and, on occasion, even doing something credible and positive. Relieved that the United States has removed its two greatest security threats, the Taliban in Afghanistan and Saddam Hussein in Iraq, Iran ponders how it might replace American political and military dominance with its own.

Iraq as Meeting Place

For the United States, attacking and occupying Iraq was all about ending terrorism, eliminating weapons of mass destruction, removing an evil and repressive dictator and liberating the Iraqi people. The war was justified by the Bush administration as part of the global war on terrorism against al-Qaida and as the only way to eliminate Saddam's weapons of mass destruction before he shared them with terrorists such as Osama bin Laden and the al-Qaida affiliates responsible for the attacks on New York City and the Pentagon on 11 September 2001. The real reason for the war was regime change in Iraq for motives that may never be known.

The administration's claims that Baghdad possessed unconventional weapons and was perhaps only a year away from having a nuclear device have proved to be false.[1] It, and previously the Clinton administration, failed to heed statements made by defectors, including Saddam's son-in-law Hussein Kamal, who headed the ministry in charge of WMD (weapons of mass destruction) programmes and defected to Jordan in 1995. It ignored information elicited by family members of Iraqi scientists sent to Iraq before the war in order to question relatives about the status of WMD research and development programmes.

The information alleging Iraqi support for al-Qaida was even more specious. The intelligence community warned the administration that the 'evidence' of Saddam supporting Osama bin Laden and al-Qaida was unsubstantiated, unreliable and illogical. The administration disregarded all criticism, claiming that the war against Iraq would be a war of liberation, not occupation, that the US and coalition forces would be welcomed with rice and rose petals and that a democratic Iraq would quickly become an example for emulation throughout the region.

With Saddam's removal from power in 2003, the Bush administration and most Iraqis had high expectations that freedom would solve all problems and bring security, stability, a transparent and fair political process, guarantees of human rights in a civil society and democratic institutions. Although most Iraqis – Sunni and Shia, Arab and Kurd, Turkmen and Christian – were grateful for American intervention removing a hated and feared dictator, liberation rapidly became occupation; and the American hold on power, but not necessarily its presence, quickly came to be resented and mistrusted.

That the United States lacked information about the state of Iraqi society and its economic infrastructure and had not prepared adequately for the 'day after' became evident in a short time. Moreover, its errors of judgement soon created an environment and an administration in Iraq that was unable to deal effectively with the looting and sabotage that began with the collapse of central authority and blossomed within months into a full-blown insurgency. Successor interim governments, from the Governing Council, appointed by the head of the Coalition Provisional Authority (CPA) Paul Bremer and dominated by prominent exiles, to the Shia-dominated government elected in January 2005, made ineffective attempts to deal with insurgent violence and other challenges to their authority. Their inability to take decisive action in fighting the insurgents and terrorists, their reluctance to assume responsibility for their actions and their inability to think other than in terms of family, clan, tribe, militia and personal self-interest caused the security situation to deteriorate further while US forces focused on finding the elusive weapons of mass destruction and rooting out terrorists.[2]

Although American and Iraqi officials tried to downplay expectations, with each election and with the approval of the constitution in October

2005, the popular perception of Iraqis and Americans was that now the violence would end, the security situation would improve, the streets would be safe and standards of living would rise. But elections, a constitution and even the capture of Saddam Hussein in December 2003 failed to halt the violence, to end the insurgencies or to provide jobs and security for Iraqis. The streets remained unsafe and the borders unsecured, allowing more terrorists, extremists and arms to enter an unguarded Iraq.

For Iran, the war in Iraq has really been about Iran and regime change in the so-called 'axis of evil'. It was not about taking revenge on Saddam for his refusal to comply with UN and American-imposed sanctions, nor was it about the West's greed for oil, protecting Israel and the United States' insistence on being hegemon of the Gulf region, just like preceding European colonial powers. Although these are 'politically correct' justifications for popular consumption on the so-called Iranian and Arab street, they failed to address Iran's real dilemma – how to avoid similar regime change in Tehran. Saddam Hussein's Iraq, even after its forced expulsion from Kuwait in 1991, the removal of most of its nuclear weapons programmes by 1997 and its loss of control of its Kurdish provinces, was still seen as a formidable threat to an Iran suffering from a devastated, war-torn economy. The US attack on Iraq now eliminated the most serious threat to the survival of an independent Iran; its territory, the Islamic revolution and the republic remained intact. (That the new Islamic Republic had threatened Iraq and its Arab neighbours in the 1980s with the export of its revolution to Shias and radicalized Arabs outside its borders was irrelevant by the 1990s.)

The American presence in Iraq serves Iranian interests in other ways. Iranian leaders can use the image of the US military occupation of Iraq and the popular apprehension that the next target for regime change is Iran to rally popular support around a beleaguered regime. This is not just a threat to the Islamic Republic; it is a threat to 2,500 years of Persian history and modern Iranian nationalism. More to the point, America's insistence on the establishment of democratic institutions, practices and values has turned power in Iraq over to the 60 per cent of the population that is Shia Muslim and that has common family and tribal as well as sectarian interests with Iran. Clerics of Iranian origin dominated Shia religious institutions and leadership positions in Iraq's Shia shrine cities of Najaf and Karbala for hundreds of years until they were expelled by Saddam in the 1970s and 1980s. Now, many Iranians saw themselves in charge again once, replacing Saddam's loyalists and appointees to the mosques there and in Baghdad. Iranian clerics have begun moving back to Iraq's shrine cities and teaching in the seminaries, buying land around Najaf in particular. Iranian students and scholars of Shia Islam are returning to study while Iranian entrepreneurs – clerical and secular – are investing in community development, construction and trade. From Iran's perspective, it has finally won its war with Iraq, and it will shape the future of Iraq and the region.

An Iraqi Perspective

Iraqis, of course, have very different perspectives on who controls their fate and why. Grateful for American help in removing Saddam but wary of American intentions, they are unsure of Iran's motives in supporting post-Saddam democracy in Iraq and concerned that the United States might leave Iraq before it is able to defend itself from internal unrest and external pressure. Their specific perspectives on America and Iran are of course coloured by who they are and what their position is in the new Iraq.

For Iraq's Kurds, the American-led war was welcome revenge on a hated regime and, for many, the first step on the way to an autonomous if not independent state. The major Kurdish factions – the Kurdish Democratic Party, led by Masud Barzani, and the Patriotic Union of Kurdistan, led by Jalal Talabani – were well known in Washington, as were their squabbles and long-term inability to cooperate. Anxious to protect their gains in Iraq's three predominantly Kurdish provinces, however, they have turned their cooperation with and support for America into its tacit acquiescence to their demand for self-rule.

Iraq's Shia population presents a much more complicated picture. Those loyal to extremist religious factions – in particular the Iran-based Supreme Council for the Islamic Revolution in Iraq (now called the Supreme Islamic Council of Iraq), led by the late Ayatollah Muhammad Baqr al-Hakim and his brother Abd al-Aziz, and the Dawa Party, Iraq's oldest Shia dissident faction, established by Ayatollah Muhammad Baqr al-Sadr in the 1960s – had joined other exiles and supported the American war on Saddam. They almost certainly assumed America's endorsement of Iraqi democratic processes, including open and transparent elections that would bring them to power; Iranian support for their ambitions to build popular support for their governance; and the backing of the *hawza*, the senior Shia clerical leaders in Najaf. They were led by Grand Ayatollah Ali Sistani, a cleric born in Iran, who urged Iraq's Shias to vote for the SCIRI- and Dawa-led coalition in the January 2005 election. They saw America's role in Iraq as temporary, and they also saw it as beneficial because it enabled them to organize politically, to elect a government that they could dominate and to buy time to consolidate their control while the US forces dealt with the post-Saddam insurgencies and violence.

Initially uncertain about what American control in Iraq would mean for them, Iraq's Sunnis soon had reason to worry. The first two acts of the CPA's head Paul Bremer ordered the demilitarization and the de-Baathification of Iraq, acts the Sunni Arabs interpreted as intending them for disenfranchisement and second-class status in the new Iraq. American efforts to ensure equal participation for all elements of Iraqi society were seen as efforts to rob the Sunni Arab community of its historic role in dominating Iraq's political and military institutions.

The CPA's efforts to make Iraqi political and military institutions more inclusive had the opposite result. Instead of incorporating Iraq's many sects and ethnic groups into a cooperative amalgam, its insistence on a mathematically correct representation – 55 to 60 per cent of posts to the assumed 60 per cent of the population that is Shia Arab, 20 per cent for Sunni Arabs, 20 per cent for the Kurds and five per cent for 'others' (including Turkmen, Armenians and Assyrian Christians) – merely reinforced the differences important to exile groups. It disregarded Iraq's identity as the majority of Iraqis described it: 'Who are you?' 'I am an Iraqi.' The exception, of course, was the Kurdish group, whose answer to the identity question was simply 'I am a Kurd.'

Growing Risks and Diminishing Opportunities for America
The United States is credited with bringing democracy to Iraq, but it is also blamed for its consequences. Many in Iraq may agree with the judgement of Iraq's Sunni Arab neighbours that the United States may even have intended from the beginning of the war to bring 'democracy' to Iraq in order to bring the Shias to power and create a permanently weakened Iraqi state. Initially, American policy-makers were convinced

that Iraq would quickly adopt democratic standards, institutions and values. Instead, politically ambitious Iraqis began squabbling for control of lucrative concessions while remnants of Saddam's military and internal security forces, demobilized Sunni military officers, jihadist religious extremists and criminal gangs seeking loot and plunder launched the insurgencies and violence that continue to beset Iraq. Ministries and positions in government were seen by some new to power as fiefdoms whose riches were to be dispensed to the loyal and favoured few, a system honoured by Saddam and now theirs.

By 2006, the expectations of American officials were much less clear. The United States appeared to see growing risks and diminishing opportunities in Iraq. Holding the first open elections in a country that had voted 99 per cent for anything Saddam had asked for did not seem to be a realistic exercise, yet it was. Iraqis were quick to display the political skills necessary for organizing political factions and negotiating deals. However, the election in January 2005 posed special and potentially destabilizing problems. The Sunni Arab threat to boycott the election worried many, who said that if the Sunnis did not accept the process, it would fail. The Sunni Arabs' ploy to get the election postponed and intimidate potential voters was intended as a demonstration of their ability to play a spoiler role. It failed. And the pictures televised by Al Jazeera must have been as riveting for Iraq's neighbours as they were for Americans.

But insofar as US policy-makers expected that elections would produce a functioning democratic political system and a pro-American government, they were disappointed. In January 2005 and again in December 2005, Iraqis voted according to their communities' perceived interests and needs, not according to the 'national interest'. In both elections, Shia political parties won the majority of the vote but not enough of a majority to give them full control. And in both elections, the Shia factions found themselves in need of alliances with Kurdish or other groups if they were to have the ability to control legislation and run the government.

The distribution of the vote in Iraq's two parliamentary elections tells an important story. In the January election, the leading Shia parties received less than 50 per cent of the vote, giving them control of 140 seats in the new parliament. The Kurdish grouping received 35 per cent of the vote, much more than the number of Iraqi Kurds warranted, and 75 seats. Sunni factions, hurt by their leaders' demand that they boycott the January election, received only 15 per cent of the vote and 17 seats. In the December election, in which approximately 70 per cent of eligible Iraqis and many Sunnis participated, Shia parties won 128 seats, Kurdish parties 55 seats and Sunni Arabs 55 seats (35 per cent of the vote, divided between Iyad Alawi's secular bloc and other Sunni Arab nationalist elements).[3]

What do these figures tell us? They say that voting as a coherent body, whether ethnic or sectarian, works. Minority parties, those not affiliated with more powerful individuals or interests or those with a small secular base, lost out. Parties with a religious affiliation or supporting Islam as part of governance are more popular than avowedly secular parties. As in most states with transparent elections, people voted according to their interests and the interests of their community, clan and family. Sunni Arabs' participation in the second election doubled their seats in the parliament and increased their influence in the government.

The issue of American influence in Iraq is likely to be overstated by Iranians and by Iraqis seeking popularity and a political future. Most Iraqis remain grateful that the United States intervened to rid Iraq of a tyrant. But liberation and gratitude for it are short-lived. They quickly turn to occupation and to impatience that all problems are not solved simply with the removal of the leader. Fear of the present and uncertainty about the future, unrealistic expectations and unmet promises soon turn people against even the most benevolent of occupiers, and America has not been a consistently benign force in Iraq. Iraqis had high expectations of what the United States would bring to their country. They expected security, jobs, improved standards of living, and punishment for their Ba'thist oppressors. Many American and other foreign NGOs and humanitarian organizations sent to help reconstruct Iraq quickly found themselves enmeshed with greedy people waiting for opportunities, returned exiles expecting to be leaders and a rapidly growing insurgency. Unmet Iraqi expectations have been used by the extremist Shia cleric Muqtada al-Sadr, who led two anti-American militia assaults in 2004, including one in Najaf. With more than 30 loyalists in the new Iraqi parliament, he hoped to shape Iraq's relations with the United States and Iran. However, even al-Sadr contradicts himself: he wants American and coalition military forces out of Iraq as soon as possible but even he has not always been willing to call for their immediate withdrawal.

Diminishing Risks and Growing Opportunities for Iran

Iran sees minimal risks and great opportunities in Iraq. It sees a friendly government run by loyal allies, many of whom lived long years of exile in Iran and others who were careful to cultivate an Iranian connection. Iranian money for investment, reconstruction, trade and humanitarian assistance is flowing into Iraq, as are pilgrims, clerics, diplomats and other government officials, traders, intelligence personnel, students and extended family members eager to return. Grateful to American forces for removing its two major external sources of threat, Iran now believes that the United States is bogged down in Iraq and Afghanistan and will be unable to fashion an exit strategy without Iranian assistance.

However, Iraq is a risk as well as an opportunity. Iraq and Iran share a 1,400-km border without border guards or monitoring. Since the fall of Saddam and of the Taliban in Afghanistan, Iran has seen a dramatic increase in drugs and arms smuggling and terrorist infiltrators on the way to or from Iraq. Just as elections did not guarantee the election of a pro-American government, so too they will not always guarantee Tehran a regime in Baghdad that is friendly towards it. Many Iraqis – Sunni Arabs, religious Shias who are members of the former exile factions that sheltered in Iran and secular Iraqis – see Iran behind every decision of the al-Jaafari and al-Maliki governments. (Nuri al-Maliki was chosen to be prime minister by the dominant Shia parties in early 2006 after al-Jaafari was rejected for a full four-year term.) Many Iraqis, regardless of sect, believe that the 'turbans are in power', directing the government's actions and turning Iraq into a theocratic state subordinate to Iran's political mullahs. They accuse Iran of infiltrating the security and intelligence services, training the police and militia units and in general undermining Iraq's independence. Others see Iran as helping with the country's reconstruction by way of trade, investment and other forms of direct and indirect assistance, but Iranian gain from Iraqi need will not create supporters for Tehran or ease its security concerns.

The truth is probably less extreme than either side depicts it, but it is still a worrisome picture. Tehran clearly provided the Shia-led government of Ibrahim al-Jaafari with much advice, financial, military and training assistance, and policy 'guidance'. The large number of pilgrims, clerics, merchants, truck-drivers, intelligence officers and students crossing into or moving back from Iraq's southern region affect its development and perception of Iran, and not all these developments are positive. Iraq's Shias are Arab, not Persian in origin, and many are uncomfortable with the kind of cleric-dominated governance they see in Iran. Iraq has no history of clerical involvement in politics, and Grand Ayatollah Sistani, born in Iran, who is Shia Islam's most senior cleric, publicly opposes clerics serving in parliament.

Sistani is indeed a major cause of concern for Iran's political clerics, according to Iranian scholars. He rejects Khomeini's principle of *velayat-i faqih* (rule by the supreme cleric or jurisprudent), and allegedly there are millions of Shias in Iran and worldwide who follow him as their *mujtahid*, the voice of authority. Many observers of Iranian and Iraqi religious rivalries claim that there is competition between the Iraqi cities Najaf and Karbala, Shia Islam's two most holy sites in Iraq, with the ancient Iranian city of Qom, the seat of its pre-eminent clerics. This claim is probably unwarranted. Najaf's importance as the burial place of Imam Ali and Karbala's significance as the burial site of his son Imam Hussein guarantee that these two cities have a place in Shia Islamic tradition, history, culture, education and folklore that no other city can surpass. Moreover, Iranian clerics, many of whom had been forced to return to Iran by Saddam Hussein in the late 1970s and early 1980s, are returning to Iraq and resuming their studies and places in the seminaries and religious courts of law. In fact, Iran may be concerned that clerics unhappy with the Supreme Leader, Ayatollah Ali Khamenei, and the clerical hard-liners running Iran will set up a base in the Iraqi shrine cities from which they might criticize the Islamic Republic.

Iran, then, has several issues to resolve in its relations with a newly friendly Iraq. Seeing a weak country, Iranian leaders will surely be tempted to seek the reparations from Baghdad for the 1980–8 war that were promised under UNSCR 598. They also want Baghdad to reaffirm its commitment to the 1975 Algiers Accord. It was signed by then Vice President Saddam Hussein and the Shah of Iran, and in it Saddam conceded to Iran territory and control over the shared Shatt al-Arab waterway in return for the Shah ending his support for Iraq's rebellious Kurds. Should Tehran insist that Baghdad complies with these demands, it could destabilize the most pro-Iranian government likely to be elected in Iraq.

In the short term, Iran appears to have little to worry about in Iraq. Stability of relations between the two states is not an issue: any government in Baghdad will need stable and positive relations with

Tehran. But a government making concessions to Iran on reparations or territory risks losing domestic support. Iraq's pro-Iranian Shia political parties will continue to win elections, but they will also lack a clear majority. Their parties did not win a clear majority in either election in 2005. Unlike the Kurds, whose two dominant factions focused their attention on one coalition, Shia Iraqis voted for the religious parties; and a small number voted for secular groupings, such as that led by the former prime minister Ayad Allawi and the Communist Party. This means that the Shia winners need to form a coalition drawn from Kurdish and/or Sunni religious parties in order to form a government. Relations with Iran were a source of division among SCIRI and Dawa factions while they were in Iranian exile. But now that they are in power, those close relations with Iran threaten to work against Shia cohesion and exacerbate tensions further between the Sunni and Shia communities in Iraq. One thing seems clear: time is not on Iran's side in Iraq.

Looking Ahead: What should Iraqis Expect?

Iraqis are understandably worried as Iran and the United States conduct direct talks in Baghdad (two meetings held in 2007 and others anticipated). The Iranians have not indicated whether Iraq will be an item for discussion, will be excluded from it or will be part of a grand bargain in which all issues are put on the table. Some Iraqis may suspect that Washington is prepared to allow Iran a free rein in Iraq in exchange for acquiescing to its exit strategy from Iraq. Other Iraqis may assume that they will take part in any US–Iran discussions because they refused to hold any meetings with Iran until their new government was in place. Since Nuri al-Maliki became prime minister in early 2006, Iran has appointed an ambassador to Baghdad, who meets with him regularly and has travelled to Tehran for talks. However, US officials say that they are determined to put an end to Iranian meddling in Iraq, including training and arming militias and encouraging civil unrest.

Removing a dictator, holding elections and even writing a constitution do not solve all problems. They do not automatically produce transparent governance, the rule of law, security, an end to violence or jobs. The only certainty is that there is no more Saddam, who was executed in December 2006. But this does not mean that a Saddam-type figure – a strong authoritarian figure able to defeat insurgents, end the violence and re-establish strong central government – will not emerge, especially if the security situation continues to deteriorate and Iraqis tire of foreign meddling, be it American, Iranian, Turkish, Saudi or other Arab. Iraqis' pride in their nationalism, history, ethnicity and faith have been underestimated and misinterpreted by many outside Iraq. And few inside or outside the country have considered the consequences of moving a diverse tribal and traditional society nearly destroyed by 35 years of terror and war into a twenty-first-century open society. Hard questions about the relationship between politics and society arise. Are tribes important or not? Is Arabism important or not? Does a Shia political majority mean the rule of clerics and an Iranian client state? And where is the much-abused Iraqi middle class?

It would be foolish to try to predict the future of Iraq or the course of its relations with Iran and America. Will Iraqis be able to define their future or to shape the direction of American–Iranian relations? Will the issue of Iran's nuclear aspirations and Western worries about its development of nuclear weapons prevent resolution of the important issue of Iraqi and regional security? Maybe and maybe not. For its part, the United States – and certainly Iran too – has much to learn about Iraq. And Tehran and Washington have much to learn about each other.

The tragedy of their relationship is that a lack of communication makes misunderstanding, resentment and fear easy and predictable. What are we afraid of? Why cannot the United States acknowledge what the Iranian government wants most: recognition, respect, acceptance and legitimacy. And why cannot Iran understand that nuclear proliferation is not a 'right' but a risk, that democracy really does mean limits on political control of civil society and human rights. How will Tehran or Washington know when a 'redline', an ultimate error in behaviour, has been crossed? If Americans do not learn to speak Farsi, visit Iran and understand its history, national insecurities and hopes for the future and if Iranians do not appreciate American or Israeli or Gulf Arab security concerns, redlines and national aspirations, how can confrontation be avoided? Americans have not been able to experience Iran since 1979; and Iran's rising generation of leaders has little knowledge or understanding of the West, in particular the United States and its democratic principles and the rule of law, the separation of powers, and checks and balances. The electoral process in the United States is hardly perfect, but I do not think that it is as obstructionist, as was seen in the 2004 Majlis election, where large numbers of potential candidates, including currently sitting members of the Majlis, were rejected for specious reasons.

A Regional Perspective

It is easy and simplistic for Iran and others to blame America's policy and presence for all the region's woes. It is said in the Gulf that 'Iraq is a mess and the United States is responsible for everything. The Americans supported Saddam; they created the war and ignored Iraq's suffering at Saddam's hands and they are the cause of the insurgencies – all to keep the region in chaos and dependent on the United States, to control the oil and to guarantee our defence budget. It is the Americans' fault that the religious extremists have joined with nationalist extremists.' Some conclude that the United States is either trying to return Sunni Arabs to power, to ensure strong-man rule, American control and an unstable region or, alternatively, to put the Shias in power in order to ensure their and Iranian control and destabilize the region. Either way, they conclude, the American occupation must end and the United States must withdraw. Then, all will be quiet, or all will be a disaster.

Three basic security issues concern Iraq's Gulf Arab neighbours. The first is about spillover from Iraq's democratic experiment and from insurgent violence. The issue is not principally about how much democracy Iraq needs. That, they say, is its business and does not affect them. Rather, the Gulf Arabs worry that as the Shias are now in charge of the government, Iraq will become a religious state dominated by Shia clerics and controlled by Iran. This could empower Shia populations in neighbouring countries living under Sunni Arab rule – from Lebanon and Syria to Saudi Arabia, Kuwait and Bahrain and on to Tajikistan – and present the possibility of a crescent of 'Shiastans'. On a deeper level, Iraq's neighbours, including Iran, may worry about the spillover effect of the distribution of power, framed by Iraq's constitution, in which there is a weak central government and most real power resides in strong, autonomous provinces, a model unwelcome in Saudi Arabia and Iran.

The second issue of concern is Iran's outspoken assumption of its natural role as regional hegemon in diplomacy, politics, trade and technology and, pre-eminently, security, all possibly to be underscored by a capability to deploy nuclear weapons. Although most of its neighbours say little publicly about the implications of a nuclear-armed or -capable

Iran, speculation is growing that Saudi Arabia, Turkey and Egypt will see a need to acquire similar capabilities, creating in Iran a sense of encirclement by Sunnis.

The third issue is dependence on the United States for security guarantees without the privilege of consultation or coordination in decisions affecting regional well-being. The Arab Gulf states would like to return to a security doctrine based on a balance of power under which they long relied on a far-away power to protect them by balancing the threat of hostile regimes in Baghdad and Tehran. They fear, however, that the United States is intent on a military confrontation with Iran, which would bring the region its fourth major war in two decades. The Gulf states will support America because they have no choice.

The policy options for the Gulf Arabs are not good. If Iraq is too weak, the risk of civil war and a spillover of terrorism and ethnic, sectarian war grows. If Iraq is too strong, the risk of new wars and/or intimidation grows because Iraq will expect to resume its 'natural leadership' in the region. The same applies to a weaker or strengthened Iran. If either country 'fails' or is consumed by civil war, the Gulf becomes a much more dangerous place. A resurgent oil-rich Iraq could remember past tensions with its small and vulnerable neighbours and begin a military build-up, which could include weapons of mass destruction programmes, especially if Iran has them. Saudi Arabia, Kuwait, Bahrain, Qatar, the United Arab Emirates and Oman, the members of the Gulf Cooperation Council, see no need to invite Baghdad or Tehran to become members, and some may even resent having to bail Iraq out of its financial woes.

A Final Word on Iraq

Several considerations are important in thinking about the role of Iran and America in Iraq, political participation there and regional security cooperation.

Identity matters. What is Iraq and who is an Iraqi? Will Iraq become a place where one's identity is Iraqi, Kurdish-Iraqi or Arab-Iraqi rather than Kurd, Arab or Turkmen? What role will tribal identity, urbanization and religion play in future identity issues?

Democracy is a process, not an event. Can it be guaranteed that elections are fair and a visible proof of democracy? Does election plus

Shia majority equal clerical governance and pro-Iranian government? The answer to both questions is a resounding no.

Legitimacy comes from responsible and effective governance, not from a political deal or a gun. A legitimate government acts on behalf of all Iraqis, not just some Iraqis. The most critical issues it would need to resolve are local security and personal safety. This means safe streets, secure jobs and the continuous availability of electricity, clean water and fuel for homes, offices and the means of transportation. Other issues are important but a little less immediate: determining the role of Islam as a basis of law, the nature of federalism, a veto for regional governments and responsibility for maintaining the rule of law and a fair and equitable system of justice.

Can there be close ties with the United States and *independence from it?* Close relations with the United States are a necessity for the current government. A critical measure of the government's independence is whether or not it is perceived as a partner rather than a client of the United States, one that is able to tell the Americans when to back off and when to proceed. What happens if Baghdad asks America to set a timetable for withdrawal? And what happens if the US government sets a timetable for withdrawal without the agreement of Baghdad?

Can Iraq 'rewrite' its history in the region? How Iraqis see themselves interacting with their neighbours in the Gulf will be a critical issue. And here, we must take a hard and honest look at what the Iraqis assume and what the Gulf states fear. When the Iraqis put their political squabbling behind them – and they will – and when they have a government that is more firmly grounded and on a more equal footing with their neighbours – and they will – then I believe two developments are inevitable. First, Iraqis will see themselves as first among equals in the Gulf and entitled to a dominant role in its political, security and strategic issues. Second, they will see the acquisition of WMD, especially a nuclear capability, as necessary to their security, sovereignty and national well-being. This will be true especially if Iran continues on its present course towards acquiring nuclear arms and long-range missiles.

What are the Dangers of a Failed Iraq?

Failure to stabilize Iraq and secure a government moving towards democratic governance will be a serous setback for the United States and Iran. Iraq will become what some said, wrongly, it was under Saddam. He was a state-sponsor of terrorism, but not of the kind that Iraq must deal with today. A failed state in Iraq could resemble the failed state Afghanistan, where the power vacuum was filled by extremists intent on a repressive and regressive form of governance and where terrorists had a safe haven and a base from which to recruit, train and launch operations against neighbouring states. For those who see America's presence as sufficient cause for rising religious militancy and terror, these would exist with or without that presence. To believe otherwise is to deny the reality of what Osama bin Laden sees as his destiny. Some in the region believe that US policy will have failed if the Shia majority in Iraq encourages similar demands from Shia minority communities in Sunni Arab-led governments. To believe this is to deny the impact of the Iranian revolution, events in Lebanon and the fall of Saddam – all these events have contributed to the growing 'awakening' of Shias and their demand for empowerment in the countries ringing Iraq and the Gulf.

Time is not on the side of Tehran or Washington. While both sides slowly consider how to resolve their differences in Iraq, events in Iraq continue to spiral out of control. The following policy recommendations are applicable for Iran, the United States and Iraq's other neighbours:

Do not meddle in Iraqi affairs. Supporting insurgents, arming the opposition, tolerating the passage of extremists through your territory with money and arms will only breed anger and mistrust among the Iraqis and buy no friends.

Help in reconstruction. Help is not just an act of charity; it is also a way to regularize contacts. The resumption of trade and business as usual will do more to help the innocent than to aid insurgents.

Recognize the legitimately elected government and support efforts to stabilize Iraq. A divided Iraq will help no one: it will not quell unrest, end insurgencies or ensure your security.

Accept the presence of Iraq and Iran in regional security discussions and organizations. For the United States, this means participating in discussions with the Iranian government. For Iran, it means

[52]

participating in transparent discussions without conditions or exclusions. For the neighbours of Iraq and Iran, this does not mean accepting either of them into the GCC, but it does mean finding a venue for resolving tensions that will inevitably arise again over borders, oil exploration and exploitation, refugees and other security issues.

Looking Back, Looking Ahead

Since the collapse of Saddam Hussein's regime in April 2003, the course of relations between Iran and the United States and between Iran and Europe and political conditions in Iran itself have grown much more complicated and contradictory. Does Tehran really reject all discourse with the 'Great Satan', or only that which it cannot control? Is the United States really sincere in offering to talk to Iran in Baghdad, or is it waiting for all other channels, through the European Union and the United Nations for example, to fail? The contacts held in 2007 shed little light on American or Iranian assumptions or expectations. Do the Iranians really insist on placing all issues on the table, or will they continue to insist that some of them, such as Iraq and their nuclear aspirations, remain off the agenda and non-negotiable? Will Washington overcome its distaste for the 'unelected' regime in Tehran and hold talks with a member of the 'axis of evil', or does it perceive real limits to its theoretical objections to the Islamic Republic? How one answers these questions reflects one's basic hopes and fears about Iran, Iraq and their neighbours. If one believes that President Ahmadinejad does not represent the consensus of Iran's policy-makers, then his anti-American, anti-Israeli rhetoric may be irrelevant.

Iraq is critical to this potential dialogue. If one accepts Iran's assumptions about its ability to contain and control Iraq, then the balance of power in the region will have changed dramatically. If, however, one believes that Tehran's assumptions about its control and influence in Baghdad are exaggerated, then it is easier to let Iran spend its treasure and energy with little worry about its success in winning Iraqi hearts and minds. At bottom, the issue is not the end of the journey; it is the journey itself.

NOTES

1 Khidr Hamza, an Iraqi nuclear scientist who fled Iraq in 1995 with the help of Ahmad Chalabi, testified in a Congressional hearing in November 2002 that Iraq was only one year away from having a nuclear device. He was wrong, but the question remains, did he deliberately mislead the American public or did he believe his story? See Khidr Hamza, *Saddam's Bombmaker* (New York: Scribners, 2001).

2 The body of memoirs and accounts by journalists of the war and the Coalition Provisional Authority grow daily. For a recent memoir, see L. Paul Bremer III, *My Year in Iraq: The Struggle to Build a Future of Hope* (New York: Simon and Shuster, 2006). Bremer led the CPA from May 2003 to May 2004.

3 Two Sunni religious factions received most of this vote. In addition, the Iraqi National Alliance, led by the former prime minister Ayad Allawi and comprised mostly of secular Iraqis, including former Baathists and Arab nationalists, won 25 seats. As of January 2006, it was trying to fashion a coalition in the parliament with Kurdish leaders and other minority parties.

4

Iranian–European Relations: A Strategic Partnership?

Shahriar Sabet-Saeidi

Relations between Iran and Europe developed rapidly after 1990 under the pragmatist presidents Rafsanjani and Khatami, and although tense at times, the relationship largely remained steady. However with the rise of Ahmadinejad to power in 2005 and his uncompromising position over Iran's nuclear activities as well as his unwise comments on subjects such as the Holocaust, this relative stability in relations has been significantly damaged, with major EU countries now tilting more towards the US approach to Iran. The current deadlock in negotiations with EU-3 (Germany, France and Great Britain), coupled with increasing accusations from American forces that Iran is supporting militant groups in Iraq, has undermined the relationship between Iran and Europe, which has been further damaged by European support for UN Security Council sanctions against Iran.

The period of 1990–2005 was of great importance for Iran's relations with Europe. 1990 coincided with the end of the war with Iraq and the collapse of communism, and 2005 incorporated all that followed the 11 September 2001 terrorist attacks on the United States – including regime change in Afghanistan and Iraq, both of which have had a huge impact on Iran and its environment.

In the aftermath of 11 September, Iran turned more than ever towards Europe, as it felt that the level of danger posed by the United States and its policies for the greater Middle East had increased dramatically. Those policies had moved beyond containment and now included the possibility of pre-emptive attacks and regime change. Iran was now viewed as part of an 'axis of evil' alongside Iraq and North Korea, and the US invasion of Iraq and the downfall of Saddam Hussain in 2003 was the beginning of a serious encirclement of Iran by US forces, now present on four corners of the Iranian borders. Such a significant military presence by the United States, with increased international diplomatic pressure, has produced a serious security predicament for Iran since then.

The 'clash of civilizations' is now the order of the day, and the West's united front against the danger of terrorism is helping the United States to fulfil its long-held dreams about the Middle East. Neo-conservatives in Washington no longer believe in the necessity of preserving the status quo in the Middle East and endeavour to democratize dictatorial regimes in the region and remove hostile ones like Iran, through which they believe that the flow of oil to the industrialized world will be secured. A resolution of the Arab-Israeli conflict was also on the agenda as the focal point of any future stability not only in the region but also throughout the globe, although this has since fallen by the wayside as a result of the complications of post-Saddam Iraq.[1] However, it seems that Arab regimes are resisting these pressures to open up their political systems as recent democratic elections showed a backlash with Islamist movements such as Hamas gathering momentum, which poses a threat both to these regimes as well as to immediate American interests in the region.[2]

With more American pressure on Iran for its alleged efforts to develop nuclear weapons, the negotiating role that Europe plays in this matter has given Tehran the chance to challenge America's encirclement strategy. Upon the fall in Afghanistan of its main ideological opponent, the Taliban, and the removal in Iraq of its sworn enemy Saddam Hussein, Iran started to play with the idea of being the regional superpower. However, the US military presence in both countries and the rising tension between Iran and the United States over Iran's activities in Iraq have made Iran more vulnerable than ever. Although Iran has been successful in establishing good relations with both governments in Baghdad and Kabul, the American pressure on these governments and against the Iranian presence has significantly affected Iran's role. Exposure to these threats has endangered Iran's interests and has made it frustrated with the new regional order.

Since 2001, US plans for political and economic reform in the Middle East have presented Iran with both opportunities and challenges. Iran is now able to influence Islamist movements throughout the region to gain power in the more open political atmosphere, and thus spread its influence within pro-American states in the region. But this is also a challenge per se which, together with the security threats, has necessitated that Iran, although active in the defence of its interests on the political, military and intelligence fronts in Iraq and Afghanistan, builds up more strategic partnerships so as to confront these threats. This partnership is meant to secure Iran's economic and security interests and to minimize the effects of US intervention in its immediate environment. Europe appeared to the Iranian political elite to be the sole partner in the West in its confrontation with the United States. However President Ahmadinejad changed this policy with a stronger interest in Latin America, Russia and China as Europe and Iran lost their mutual trust. Ahmadinejad is trying to avoid reliance on Europeans and his foreign policy apparatus is of the strong belief that Iran has missed many opportunities by ignoring African and Latin American countries and that Iran can enjoy huge benefits from alliances with the East.[3] As a result, the Iranian government has been trying to build stronger links with these countries; however, most of them have failed to prevent further pressure on Iran because they lack the necessary means and are also not ready to sacrifice their own interests in a battle between Iran and the United States.

This chapter reviews Iran's relations with Europe since the presidency of Rafsanjani and examines Europe's response to Iran's attempts to improve them. It scrutinizes the idea that Europe is Iran's strategic partner in the West and that this partnership provides Iran with the necessary economic and political support it needs. This is an attempt to attract further discussion and research on the subject and challenge the idea of the significance of Europe to Iran.

Iran–Europe Relations Under Rafsanjani: The Enemy Within

Akbar Hashemi Rafsanjani became president in 1989 amid high tensions between Iran and the European countries because of the fatwa issued against Salman Rushdie. This had led to the withdrawal of European ambassadors from Tehran, the cancellation of some high-level visits to Iran and Iran's reciprocal withdrawing of its ambassadors.

However, Rafsanjani soon introduced a policy of détente, to end Iran's isolation in the international community in the so-called 'era of reconstruction'. This policy had a clear economic orientation, as Iran sought foreign investment and loans for the government's ambitious economic plans. The 'second republic'[4] was the start of pragmatism in Iran's foreign policy and an end to a decade of ideological stand-off with the West and Arab countries. Iraq's invasion of Kuwait in 1990 in particular gave Rafsanjani the opportunity for *rapprochement* with the Persian Gulf Arab states as well as for opening doors to Europe. As Ehteshami has pointed out, Iran's neutralist stance and its support for the UN position on the Iraqi invasion of Kuwait was a clear sign of the new policy.[5]

This policy brought an immediate response from European countries in 1990: they removed economic sanctions against Iran and normalized relations with it. Iran then took further steps, securing the release of the Western hostages in Lebanon and permitting the United Nations Special Representative on Human Rights to visit the country for the first time since the Revolution. There followed visits by the foreign ministers of Germany and France, the first official European visits to Iran since the Revolution; and trade relations began to develop, even though the Rushdie affair haunted bilateral relations with Britain. However, the assassination of Shapour Bakhtiar, the last Shah's prime minister, in Paris in 1991 and also of Kurdish opposition leaders in Berlin in 1992 (the 'Mykonos incident', named after the restaurant where they were dining) dashed Rafsanjani's hopes for better relations with Europe.

It was later revealed that a radical wing of Rafsanjani's administration had consistently tried to thwart his attempts to normalize relations with the West by mounting political assassinations abroad and articulating extremist views towards the West at home. Rafsanjani himself was not able to respond efficiently to European concerns about Iran's human rights record or on the matter of the fatwa against Rushdie. The European governments' desire to maintain relations with Iran, on the one hand, and the persistence of tension, on the other hand, led them to launch a new, unified policy of 'critical dialogue' with the Islamic Republic.

'Critical Dialogue'

In December 1992, the policy of 'critical dialogue' was announced at the European Council in Edinburgh. It raised four concerns with respect to Iran: the abuse of human rights, the fatwa against Rushdie, arms procurement by Iran and its approach to the Arab–Israeli peace process – all issues which remain a focal point of tension between not only Iran and Europe but specially between Iran and the United States (with the exception of the Rushdie affair, which was resolved under Khatami). For the most part, Europe's approach to these concerns concentrated on

Iran's human rights issues. However, this trend has changed within the last couple of years with a successful US agenda to magnify Iran's threat and its nuclear activities.

Under 'critical dialogue', no significant improvements were made on human rights, and at the same time the United States put pressure on Europe by way of economic sanctions against Iran. This included any foreign investment of more than $40 million per year in oil and gas projects, which was mainly because European countries continued to invest in Iran, replacing American investors in Iran and making American sanctions ineffective. During this period there was no progress on the Rushdie affair: although Iran did not make any attempt to carry out the fatwa, it still did not vow to abandon it either. There was also no serious friction over Iran's weapons programmes or Iran's support for Islamist movements in the region, which Europeans saw as an obstacle towards peace in the Middle East. This period saw hopes for a steady, normal relationship with Europe, although these hopes were later dashed by a series of negative developments.

When arrest warrants were issued by a German court against high-level Iranian officials, including Rafsanjani himself in connection with political assassinations, all European ambassadors were recalled from Tehran. With the suspension of 'critical dialogue', relations between Iran and the European Union came to a halt.

'Critical dialogue' hardly succeeded, but it was more effective than the US policy of 'dual containment', which was based on isolating Iran and Iraq through political, economic and military means. The policy announced in 1993 was conceptualized by Martin Indyk, the then Middle East officer of the National Security Council, and was later developed by Anthony Lake, Special Assistant to President Clinton for National Security. In an article for *Foreign Affairs* Lake laid down the foundations of this new policy, which was based on the concept that Iran and Iraq posed serious threats to the interests of the United States and stability in the region. He argued that with the end of the Cold War there was no longer any role for them to play in the rivalries of superpowers and also emphasized the importance of the free flow of oil in the Persian Gulf. To secure both US interests and the stability of the region he recommended the policy of 'dual containment', which could only be achieved through regional allies of the United States, which were gathered in the [Persian] Gulf Cooperation Council.[6]

The United States did not succeed in convincing the European Union to join its embargo on Iran, which mainly banned American companies from investing in Iran's oil and gas sectors. American companies suffered big losses after President Clinton's Executive Order in 1995 as Iran turned to Europe, whose companies became its biggest partner in trade and technology. For example, the French company Total soon replaced the American company Conoco when President Clinton banned it from investing in Iranian oilfields. The second phase of American sanctions came under the Iran–Libya Sanctions Act of 1996 (ILSA) by which the United States tried to impose secondary sanctions against foreign companies investing in Iran's petroleum sector. However, the European Union responded with strong legislation preventing European companies and citizens from complying with ILSA.

Patrick Clawson, a well-known critic of European policies, argued at the time that there were 'three major points of disagreement' between the policies of the United States and the European Union towards the Islamic Republic – about commerce, geostrategy and reinforcing the moderates. He rejected the EU vision that Iran was an important commercial partner of Europe and argued that Europe and Japan considered Iran to be the same important partner that it had been during the 1970s but that Iran under Rafsanjani was a declining economy and in a debt crisis.

He also argued that Iran's geostrategic importance had decreased because its 'oil fields are old and its reserves expensive to develop' and 'the price of oil is set far more at the commodity exchanges than by decisions of the Organization of Petroleum Exporting Countries. Political friendships no longer have their former value. Therefore, a special relationship with Iran matters little for oil security.'[7]

Clawson also refuted the idea that Iran was an important and influential player in the Muslim world. Although parts of the Islamic Revolution's message were welcomed in the Muslim world, 'Iran has limited influence over the Muslim world and non-Persian Sunnis are not about to follow any Iranian cleric', he argued. Finally, he contended, there was no chance for moderate politics in the country. Iranian politicians neither cared about the outside world – they concentrated on domestic politics – nor felt any necessity to change 'their policies to secure what they want from the major powers'. This was because they believed that Europe and Japan 'will continue trade and investment irrespective of Iranian actions because of Iran's importance as an oil supplier and as a market'.[8]

In comparing US and EU policies towards Iran, Struwe makes a very precise analysis of the 'critical dialogue' policy. The European Union's approach to Iran, he suggests, had two major characteristics: first was its consideration of 'Iran's domestic position' and its refusal 'to punish the state of Iran collectively'. Secondly, 'the EU remained opposed to any measures contradicting international law' and, contrary to the United States, it never 'perceived Iran as an outlaw state'. Instead, it was a country 'that had to be persuaded, not bullied, to respect the norms and principles it has signed up to'.[9]

Within Europe however, the European Parliament opposed the 'critical dialogue' approach, especially after the Mykonos trial verdict in 1997, when it called on the Council to end it and to 'enhance the dialogue with those promoting the transformation of Iran into a democratic state'.[10] The European Parliament plays a central role on issues related to human rights. Concerns about the situation of human rights in Iran and strong lobbying by Iranian opposition groups in Europe led the European Parliament to make human rights a key part of the 'critical dialogue'[11] and it closely followed developments. The European Parliament put pressure on other European bodies so that its concerns were addressed properly within the 'critical dialogue' as a multi-dimensional policy.

Iran–EU Relations under Khatami: A New Start

Mohammad Khatami's accession to the presidency in 1997 was the beginning of not only a new phase in Iran's foreign policy but also a fundamental change in the political discourse of the Islamic Republic. His reformist policies brought new hopes for a nation disappointed with Rafsanjani and a country isolated from the West. Fresh efforts were made to mend fences with the West in the framework of the new foreign policy.

Khatami's foreign policy was based on three fundamentals: dignity, wisdom and prudence; détente in foreign relations; and dialogue among civilizations.[12] The core of his policy was détente, which was aimed mainly at Arab states and the West. Relations with neighbouring Arab countries did improve very quickly, especially those with Saudi Arabia. The *rapprochement* with Saudi Arabia did help the two countries to secure the oil market for their interests through OPEC; and for the first time since its establishment in 1960, the target 'price limits' were defined and a mechanism was developed to guarantee this limit.[13] Khatami's successful presidency of the Organization of the Islamic Conference for four years was an excellent opportunity for him to start eliminating tensions between Iran and the Arab world and he successfully developed relationships during his presidency. The signing of a security pact with Saudi Arabia in 2001 was another step towards Iran's ultimate goal of pushing extra-regional forces out of the Persian Gulf, although this goal was not achieved.

However, Arab states have never been regarded as strategic partners for Iran mainly because most of these countries do not enjoy an important role on the international scene, they are not strong economic powers and Shiite Iran does not necessarily have many things in common with Sunni countries. So strategically, Iran needed to look to the West to secure its economic and political interests.

The roots of this argument lay in the economic malaise of Iran and the need for immediate economic aid and foreign investment in order to advance the post-war reconstruction plans that were started by President Rafsanjani but were only half-finished or suffered technical difficulties. As Sariolghalam argues, the northern, southern and eastern neighbours of Iran and the Muslim world do not have the capacity and potential that Western countries can offer Iran, and, as he recommends, the Iranian elite have to reach a consensus over the country's interests and their approach toward the West.[14] The country's need for Western capital, technology and science motivated a westward look by Khatami's administration.

At the same time, Khatami was in a position to resolve the long-standing hostility between Iran and the United States in the context of détente with the West when he appeared in a rare interview with CNN and admired the 'great American nation'. He proposed the relaxation of contacts between the two countries' nationals and more academic links, an invitation which was not very much appreciated by the Clinton administration.

As mentioned earlier, Khatami became president at a time when relations between Iran and the European Union had deteriorated significantly owing to the verdict in April 1997 of the German Mykonos trial and the subsequent withdrawal of all EU ambassadors from Tehran. But with Khatami in office and his new foreign policy in the hands of the foreign minister Kamal Kharrazi, high-level meetings between the two sides took place. Finally, the ambassadors of Finland, Sweden, Denmark, Belgium, the Netherlands, Italy, Austria, Spain, the United Kingdom, Greece and Ireland returned to Tehran. The German and French ambassadors came back later and Iranian ambassadors returned to the European capitals. 'This return points to the importance of the Islamic Republic of Iran, its stability and might in the region, and there is a good future ahead of us', Khatami said on the eve of the European ambassadors' return to Tehran.[15]

Europe's response to Khatami's election was very positive, and the realistic approach it took against US policy considerably favoured the interests of the reformist camp of the Islamic Republic as the European Union started its 'constructive dialogue' with Iran in Vienna in July 1998. Dr Albert Rohan, the head of the EU delegation, made it clear that Europe was adopting a supportive policy for reform in Iran and stated that 'the dialogue was designed to strengthen the hand of the moderates led by President Khatami'. Although the reform camp had not been totally successful in its policy, as Rohan noted later, the European Union's assistance in improving the battered Iranian economy was a crucial way of helping to bolster Khatami's moderate cause.[16] When Lamberto Dini, Italy's foreign minister, paid a visit to Tehran in March 1998, he reflected the common policy of the EU member states towards Khatami when he wrote in *La Repubblica* that 'by meeting with Khatami, Italy is strengthening him domestically, thereby increasing his efforts towards moderation and improvement of human rights'.[17]

Several high-level meetings and exchanges took place between the two sides, but the most important achievement of Khatami's détente policy was the momentous meeting between Kharrazi and the British foreign secretary Robin Cook in New York on 2 September 1998. This resulted in the resumption of full diplomatic relations between Iran and the United Kingdom, the first such agreement since the 1979 Islamic Revolution.[18] The exchange of ambassadors and Kharrazi's visit to London, leading to a declaration in which the Iranian government assured the British government that it would not take any action to implement the fatwa against Rushdie, removed the principal obstacle to bilateral relations and opened a new chapter in Iran's relations with Britain.[19]

The next phase of Iran's move towards Europe was a series of visits by President Khatami, the first of their kind since the Islamic Revolution. Khatami chose Italy and France as his first European destinations in 1999. Analysts gave various reasons for the choice of those countries, but it seems that the main one was the economic importance of Italy and France to the Islamic Republic and the more stable relations with them since the revolution. Earlier, the Italian Ente Nazionale Idrocarburi SpA and the French oil company Elf signed a contract for $998 million for the development of the Dorud oilfield in the northern Persian Gulf,[20] and Italy had rescheduled $370 million of loans.[21]

A commentary in *Le Figaro* on Khatami's visit noted that

> Rome and Paris were not chosen randomly to be the first capitals of Europe where President Khatami comes in an attempt to show that Iran has changed. ELF and ENI recently signed joint, important oil contracts with Tehran. While the United States keeps its favourite practice of economic boycotting, France and Italy chose to help Iran open up, demonstrating that, for the sake of prosperity, it is possible to find links of reciprocity between the West and Iran. This approach could be seen as cynical. It nevertheless brings a theocracy to recognize that Islam is not sufficient to define Iranian interests.[22]

During Khatami's visit to France, Credit Lyonnais, Société Générale, Credit Agricole and Paribas gave Iran over $2 billion in credits, according to *L'Orient-Le Jour*. France was also trying to bring Iran's debt under Paris Club protection, which would spread the risk internationally.[23]

In Germany, Khatami secured a $550 million loan for Iran's National Petrochemical Company in June 2000 from a German-led consortium of European banks.[24] He also obtained an increase in Hermes credit risk coverage, from 200 million marks ($99 million) to one billion marks.[25]

During Khatami's visits, European officials discussed their own issues of concern with the Iranian president, including human rights, always an issue in relations with Iran, and its interference in the Middle East peace process. Even the Vatican secretary of state Cardinal Angelo Sodan brought up the controversial subject of human rights in a meeting with Khatami after the Iranian president had held talks with Pope John Paul II, an occasion regarded as 'an important, promising day' by the Pope.[26] The French too were under pressure to express their concern about Iran's human rights record, the death sentence for two Iranian students and, above all, the fate of 13 Iranian Jews arrested on suspicion of espionage for Israel. But although these issues were discussed with the Iranian president, French officials did not press him about them. As Olivier Roy believed, the French understood that 'the case of the 13 Jews is part of the ongoing contest between reformers and conservatives in Iran and that it will ultimately be resolved satisfactorily'; and they also realized that 'Iran's judiciary, which is independent and dominated by conservatives, uses legal cases to influence the government's foreign policy.'[27]

Meanwhile, political constraints came to overshadow the visits because in Iran the conservatives began to grumble about inopportune issues. For example, *Jomhuri-ye Eslami* newspaper reported that Salman Rushdie was to visit a Paris bookstore when Khatami happened to be in France. It argued that 'inviting the apostate Salman Rushdie to Paris on the eve of the Iranian president's visit is tantamount to an act of spite by the French government against the Islamic Republic'.[28]

However, Khatami successfully stressed the common interests of Iran and Europe and made his case for more support from Europe. For instance, in a meeting with the president of the French senate Christian Poncelet, he emphasized that 'the Islamic Republic of Iran has always made efforts to make the region secure and calm'; and referring to Iran's détente policy, he said that 'the policy is providing regional security'.[29] He also rejected the 'unipolar world' and emphasized the fact that Iran and France held identical views on the issue,[30] as did Poncelet, who stressed that the Islamic Republic of Iran enjoyed a special position in the multipolar world.[31]

Common Interests and Differences

Iran and Europe have many grounds for bilateral cooperation based on common interests and values. The American policy of isolating Iran and imposing sanctions on it and Khatami's failure to improve the Islamic Republic's relations with the United States has forced Iran to turn to the European countries for the advancement of its economic and political interests. The European Union has always taken a softer position towards Iran in controversial issues such as human rights and its nuclear programme. At the same time, Iran plays an important regional role, and Europe needs its help not only to secure its interests in Iraq and Afghanistan but also in Iran's wider environment. Looking eastward, for example, the danger of drugs trafficking from Afghanistan to Europe through Iran is of great importance to the EU member states and offers significant opportunities for cooperation. Iran is paying a high price in the fight against drug trafficking and hundreds of policemen are killed every year. Its close links with Iraq's Shia majority and the influence it has in Iraq suggests the necessity of engaging it in any arrangements for the Persian Gulf region. Stability and peace will be unachievable without including Iran in political and economic arrangements in its neighbourhood.[32]

In view of the recent international efforts to fight terrorism, Iran is a would-be actor in the Western camp. Because of ideological differences between Shia Iran and the Sunni Muslim world, which is a hotbed for radical Islamic extremism, the West can have the benefit of Iran's assistance in the fight against terrorism. Iran already claims that it has captured members of al-Qaida, but it is waiting for a Western response to its concerns. Although the United States leads the international coalition against terrorism, it is excluding Iran; it accuses it of harbouring terrorists and supporting international terrorism, which does not benefit the coalition. Europe, however, *can* enjoy Iran's assistance in this fight.

From the economic aspect in 2001, Iranian exports to the European Union totalled €6.7 billion; imports amounted to €6.6 billion. Eighty per cent of EU imports from Iran are oil products, thus the European Union is one of its main trading partners.[33] As mentioned earlier, Iran has signed various agreements with European countries for financial facilities and investment, and it also engages in general economic cooperation with the European Union.

However, one can spot crucial differences between Iran and the European Union that hinder further cooperation. Human rights have always been the main concern of Europe, over and above other issues such as Iran's interference in the Middle East conflict and its efforts to expand its domestic military capabilities.

During Khatami's visits to Europe, the first concern expressed by his hosts was about violations of human rights, for example restrictions on press freedom, the arrest of students and Jews and imposing the death penalty on those participating in violent unrest. According to human rights groups, the situation in Iran has not made significant progress, and groups such as Human Rights Watch and Reporters without Borders have criticized the EU policy of engagement with Iran without any reference to its human rights abuses. As a result of these pressures and the observance of EU principles, there is now a set of preconditions for further trade negotiations that Iran must fulfil.

The importance of human rights in Iran has faded recently as its nuclear development activities have come under scrutiny. The International Atomic Energy Agency (IAEA) has long paid regular visits to Iran's nuclear sites, as required by the Non-Proliferation Treaty (NPT), to which Iran is a signatory. The agency's reports were mostly positive, with no sign of dissatisfaction with Iran's plans and activities, until 2003, when it announced that Iran was attempting to enrich uranium that could be used in nuclear weapons. The announcement was badly timed, as the United States was preparing for war in Iraq, and put Iran in a difficult situation: there were threats from the United States and especially Israel, which is now within range of Iranian missiles.

The IAEA's board of governors adopted a resolution in November 2003 expressing 'deep concern that Iran has failed in a number of instances over an extended period of time to meet its obligations under its Safeguards Agreement with respect to the reporting of nuclear material, and its processing and use, as well as the declaration of facilities'. The resolution noted 'with the gravest concern' that Iran had 'enriched uranium and separated plutonium in undeclared facilities, in the absence of IAEA safeguards'. It also referred to 'a pattern of concealment resulting in breaches of safeguard obligations' and Iran's 'contradictory' provision of information. The resolution stopped just short of accusing Iranian officials of lying or of declaring Iran to have been in violation of its NPT obligations. Most importantly, it underlined Iran's agreement 'to suspend enrichment-related and reprocessing activities' and to sign the Additional Protocol, which stipulates that 'pending its entry into force, Iran will act in accordance with the provisions of that Protocol'.

Later, three EU foreign ministers, from France, Germany and the United Kingdom, made a historic visit to Tehran in order to resolve the issue while the United States was pushing the IAEA to refer the case to the Security Council. Following intensive negotiations Iran agreed:

- to engage in full cooperation with the IAEA to address and resolve, through full transparency, all requirements and outstanding issues of the agency and clarify and correct any possible failures and deficiencies within the IAEA;
- to sign the IAEA Additional Protocol and to commence ratification procedures. As a confirmation of its good intentions, the Iranian government stated that it would continue to cooperate with the agency in accordance with the protocol in advance of its ratification; and
- to suspend all uranium-enrichment and -reprocessing activities, as defined by the IAEA.[34]

Iran suspended its enrichment activities, but the situation deteriorated because it expected the European countries to help it close the case with the IAEA. However, the case was not closed and with later political developments in Iran and a more conservative government in place the situation has significantly deteriorated and the United States and specially Israel are losing patience with Iran's nuclear activities.

It is now obvious that Europe has used this opportunity to mend its differences with the United States. It is aligning itself more with the United States against Iran, and this has made Iran take a tougher position, arguing that although the West has turned a blind eye to Israel's nuclear capabilities, the international community is putting pressure on Iran.[35]

It is worth noting that even with a conservative president in Iran and closer ties between the United States and European countries, especially Germany and France, Europeans are still trying to avoid imposing unilateral sanctions against Iran and argue that any punishment against Iran needs to be implemented through the UN Security Council.

The American Dimension

The Bush doctrine, sketched by neoconservative theorists, has two main concepts: unilateralism and pre-emptive war. This has had a significant impact on the international system, especially transatlantic relations. One of the Bush doctrine's basic premises is that legitimacy comes from the US constitution and the American electorate, not from the consent of other countries or universal principles. This is the opposite of the views expressed by pro-international law countries such as France and Germany. Also, pre-emption and the use of military power are of higher priority to the United States than the diplomatic solutions endorsed and sought by Europe.

But the United States is the only dominant power in the world; and although we have observed opposition to its policies by some European powers such as Germany and France in the past, the majority of European countries try to align themselves with American policies. Apart from being an important player in trade, Europe is no longer considered to be a global power. There is a huge gap in the relative economic strength of America and Europe. For example, a recently released report points out that expenditure on information and communication technology in Europe is currently some 20 years behind that of the United States.[36]

Europeans have shown that they cannot gather their forces to confront US policies in the international arena, and they are aligning themselves with American policy in order to avoid further loss of prestige and influence.

It is a quarter of a century since diplomatic ties between Iran and the United States were broken, and Iran has put all its energy into retaining open relations with Europe despite the instability and unreliability of this relationship. It had the best economic relations with Europe under Khatami, but an observer might not conclude that this was profitable for Iran, largely because of US sanctions and limitations imposed on European countries. For example, Iran could not secure the purchase of new aeroplanes (such as the Airbus) to replace its old-fashioned air fleet during these years, and an agreement between Iran and Germany to produce Mercedes-Benz in Iran foundered because Chrysler was the main shareholder in the Mercedes-Benz Corporation.

Because European powers are moving closer to US policy on Iran and because they are unable to offer Iran major economic benefits (for example support Iran's bid to join the World Trade Organization), the negotiations on Iran's nuclear development have become harder than ever. Contrary to the Paris Agreement of 2004 between the European Union and Iran on the latter's temporary suspension of uranium-enrichment, the Europeans demanded that Iran cease all uranium-enrichment activities, which Iran did not accept and the case was finally referred to the Security Council and two rounds of sanctions were imposed against Iran in 2006–07. This change of position is a direct result of American pressure as well as Iran's new rigid foreign policy under President Ahmadinejad. As Ambassador Holbrook pointed out in an interview with CNN, Europe could not have negotiations with Iran without the US presence, and possibly America has the final say in this case.

Iran has to build strong relationships with all European countries to strengthen its political, economic, technological and security status in the international community and no other part of the world can offer more strategic opportunities to Iran than Europe. But European countries face certain deficiencies and the main problem within Europe is the lack of a coherent foreign policy. The significant divide between Britain and other European states over subjects such as the war in Iraq is also an important factor with respect to Iran. Although countries like France are adopting a tougher stance toward Iran, one still cannot trace a united policy within Europe on many subjects, including Iran. Also, many European countries such as France and Germany, with which Iran enjoys the strongest economic relations, are experiencing economic difficulties. As mentioned above, the gap between Europe and the United States in finance, technology and science is widening and Europe is no longer in a position to support the needs of a large country like Iran. Politically Europeans have long distanced themselves from events in the Middle East and the United States is running a one-man show in the region with a huge military presence on Iranian borders.

Europe is a would-be strategic partner for Iran with a significant political and economic role to play only if Iran can resolve its differences with the United States, as these differences are a major obstacle for any long-term strategic relationship between Iran and other countries. Even countries like Russia and China, which Iran relies on in many aspects, use Iran as a bargaining chip in their conflicts with the United States. It is worth mentioning that Americans well comprehend that they also do not have any realistic option in the region without Iranian support. There also remain two options for the United States, either changing the regime in Iran or engaging the Islamic Republic in its arrangements in the region. If both countries build the necessary confidence and search for common ground, many new horizons will be opened. Only under such conditions can Iran form reliable and strategic relations with other countries including Europe, despite Europe's limits in the new American-designed world order.

NOTES

1 For details on America's Middle East policy, see RAND's electronic conference proceedings, 'The United States, Europe, and the Wider Middle East', Shahram Chubin, Bruce Hoffman, William Rosenau, http://www.rand.org/pubs/conf_proceedings/2004/RAND_CF210.pdf and for Iran's post-9/11 foreign policy, consult Kaveh Afrasiabi and Abbas Maleki, 'Iran's Foreign Policy after 11 September', *The Brown Journal of World Affairs*, vol. IX, issue 2 (Winter/Spring 2003), pp. 255–65 and Anoushiravan Ehteshami, 'Iran's International Posture After the Fall of Baghdad', *The Middle East Journal*, vol. 58, no. 2 (Spring 2004), pp. 179–94.

2 In personal encounters with Jordanian and Egyptian diplomats they expressed their concerns with regard to US support for political reforms in the region and the threat it poses to the US interests and stability in the region.

3 Personal interview with Iran's deputy foreign minister for European and American affairs, Saeid Djalili, Paris, 2006.

4 The 'Second Republic' is used by Anoushiravan Ehteshami in *After Khomeini: The Iranian Second Republic* (London: Routledge, 1995) for the Islamic Republic under Rafsanjani or the post Iran–Iraq war period.

5 Ibid. p. 152.

6 Anthony Lake, 'Confronting backlash states', *Foreign Affairs,* Mar/Apr, vol. 73, issue 2, pp. 45–55.

7 Patrick Clawson, 'What to do about Iran?', *The Middle East Quarterly*, vol. II, no. 4 (December 1995), p. 43.

8 Ibid. p. 43.

9 Struwe, V. Matthiass (1998), 'The policy of "critical dialogue": an analysis of European human rights policy towards Iran from 1992 to 1997'. Durham Middle East papers; 60, Middle East and Islamic Studies, University of Durham, p. 35.

10 Ibid. p. 37.

11 Ibid. p. 11.

12 Khatami's meeting with Iranian ambassadors, ISNA news agency, 16 June 2003.

13 For further information see: Barzegar Kayhan, 'Detente in Khatami's Foreign Policy and its Impact on Improvement of Iran-Saudi Relations', *Discourse Iranian Quarterly*, vol. 2, no. 2 (Fall 2000), pp. 157–78.

14 Mahmoud Sariolghalam, *Siasat-e-Khareji-e-Jomhouri-e-Eslami-e-iran* [The Foreign Policy of the Islamic Republic of Iran] (Markaz-e-tahghighat-e-estratejik, 1370), pp. 154–8.

15 Hamid Reza Shokoohi, 'A glance at four years of foreign policy of Khatami administration', *Azma*: *Cultural, Social & Political Weekly*, no. 11 (June 2001), pp. 10–19.

16 BBC News website, 19 Dec. 1998.

17 *Iran Report*, RFE/RL, 15 March 1999, vol. 2, no. 11.

18 *Iran International*, no. 8, March 2000, pp. 89–90.

19 *Hamshahri* newspaper, 26 August 1998.

20 *Iran Report* (RFE/RL), vol. 2, no. 108, 8 March 1999.

21 *Iran Report* (RFE/RL), vol. 2, no. 11, 15 March 1999.

22 *Weekday Magazine* (RFE/RL), 11 March 1999.

23 *Iran Report* (RFE/RL), vol. 2, no. 43, November 1999. Paris Club consists of countries that provide debtor nations with solutions to repay their debt which are in different forms, such as rescheduling or reduction of debt.

24 Rferl/RL radio report, 10 July 2000.

25 *Iran Report* (RFE/RL), vol. 3, no 27, 17 July 2000.

26 *Weekday Magazine* (RFE/RL), 11 March 1999.

27 *Weekday Magazine* (RFE/RL), 27 October 1999.

28 *Jomhuri-ye Eslami*, 5 October 1999.

29 IRNA, English Service, 28 October 1999.

30 Idem.

31 Idem.

32 For Iran's role in Iraq, see the Chatham House Briefing Paper 'Iraq in Transition: Vortex or Catalyst?', Chatham House, Middle East Programme BP 04/02, September 2004, p. 12 and Anoushiravan Ehteshami, 'Iran's International Posture After the Fall of Baghdad', *The Middle East Journal*, vol. 58, no. 2 (Spring 2004), pp. 179–94.

33 See http://europa.eu.int/comm/external_relations/iran/intro/.

34 Paris Agreement, look at http://www.iaea.org/Publications/Documents/Infcircs/2004/infcirc637.pdf for full text.

35 On European–American relations concerning Iran's nuclear programme see 'More sticks, Europe!', *Die Zeit*, 18 March 2004 and 'Iran's nuclear program: The US and EU have to come together', *The International Herald Tribune*, 27 February 2004.

36 'Restoring European economic and social progress: unleashing the potential of ICT', Indepen, January 2006, http://www.indepen.co.uk/panda/docs/brt-summary.pdf.

5

Iran: Caught Between
European Union–United States Rivalry?

Anastasia Th. Drenou

This chapter discusses the background and development of America's 'dual containment' policy towards Iran and Iran's nuclear programme to 2004 and examines the stance of the European Union towards both. It will show that the European Union and the United States, regardless of any other motives, have used Iran in a prolonged rivalry on the international stage.

Following the demise of the Soviet Union in 1991, there was little doubt that the United States would take the lead in world affairs given its military, economic and technological supremacy. The United States became by default the world's only superpower, and the diminution of NATO, for instance, highlighted the American conviction that the only challenge to its hegemony worldwide had been eliminated. But the European Community's member states were starting to show signs of a unified political will and possibly a wish to take their economic union some steps further. Arguably the ultimate intention was to cease to follow unreservedly American commands on practically every international issue of importance, for example the 1990–1 Gulf war and the Balkan conflicts.

Needless to say, such a major transformation would require much time and effort, but it was already evident by the early 1990s that this was a firm resolve of European leaders. The evolution of the European Political Cooperation into the Common Foreign and Security Policy (CFSP) by way of the Treaty on European Union and the Amsterdam Treaty was the most prominent step taken until then towards political integration. The Europeans seemed to embark on a campaign to free

The author would like to acknowledge the critical feedback of Dr Andrew J. Newman and Dr Laleh Khalili on an earlier version of this chapter.

themselves from American domination and to restore Europe to 'great power' status. Consequently, they made a point of distancing themselves from US policies, particularly those towards third countries; and the case of Iran stands out as perhaps the most prominent one.

The European and American outlooks do not differ much in view of their similar civilizational identities and shared values, and neither do their interests in Iran and the Middle East differ in general. Both entities desire a politically stable Middle East without turmoil or upheavals: the first Gulf war and European and American involvement in the Middle East peace process between Israel and the Palestinian Authority are examples. Both also want to secure the uninterrupted flow of relatively cheap oil and look to Middle Eastern markets for the export of their goods and services. During the Iran–Iraq war in the 1980s, the American navy and European naval missions of minesweepers were involved in securing the uninterrupted navigation of commercial vessels in the Persian Gulf. These interests have remained more or less unchanged, especially since the end of the Cold War, but the two sides diverge notably in identifying and prioritizing the threats to their interests and the means of dealing with them. Shared historical experiences, the geographical proximity of Europe and the Middle East and the decline of European power, especially after the Second World War, have toned down the European powers' attitude towards their former colonies. On the other hand, the geographical and political isolation of the United States until the beginning of the twentieth century, its swift rise to superpower status and its experience of the Cold War account for the assertiveness and perhaps arrogance evident in its approach to the Middle East and elsewhere.

In contrast to relations between the United States and Iran, which have been fairly straightforward, principally since the Iranian revolution of 1979 and the hostage-taking at the US embassy in Tehran, relations between Europe and Iran are far more complex. The reasons for this are, as mentioned, numerous and go back in time, and it is beyond the scope of this chapter to analyse them in depth.

The unique relationship between Europe and Iran has caused the European Union to follow an approach towards it which is entirely different from that of the United States, even though more often than not the interests of the two parties in Iran seem to converge. Thus, when the United States sought to completely isolate the state that it considered a sponsor of terrorism and a threat to international and perhaps American security, the Europeans chose to consistently engage Iran in dialogue and to steadily promote their economic and political relations with the Islamic Republic.

Arguably, the motives behind this policy do not stem only from Europe's acknowledgement of the importance of Iran as a regional power or from its close historical, geographical and other ties and shared experiences. The policy seems to be more an attempt to safeguard European vested interests there and to establish a stronghold in one of the very few Middle Eastern states where American presence and influence are not prevalent. In other words, Europeans appear eager to resist American interventionism in the Middle East. However, this is most probably not because of goodwill and a desire to stand by local populations but because of a neo-Orientalist conviction that they must repossess their former colonies under the modern pretext of trade, cultural, economic and political cooperation agreements, while they disregard legitimate concerns on issues such as human rights violations, in order to rise to 'great power' status again and perhaps stand on an equal footing with the United States. Possibly, Iran offers the best grounds for Europe to contest American influence because, as highlighted above, it is one of the very few Middle Eastern countries that still declines even to consider any restoration of its relations with the United States, and it also resists fervently American hegemony in the region. In addition, it seems that Iran is eager to enter into various agreements with the European Union and willingly supplies the European continent with much-needed energy products as it welcomes European investments that boost the Islamic Republic's revenues.

By way of illustrating this point, the European Union's attitude towards Iran and the United States is examined in two cases. The first case is the Iran-Libya Sanctions Act (ILSA) and its repercussions at the end of the 1990s. The second concerns Iran's nuclear programme and the developments that took place until the Iranian presidential elections of 2005.

ILSA and Total

US firms remained heavily involved in the Iranian oil industry until 1994 despite the American government's policies and the absence of diplomatic ties between the United States and the Islamic Republic since 1980. In 1995, however, the Clinton administration cancelled a $600 million contract between Iran and Conoco for the development of the Sirri island oilfields and signed the Iran Sanctions Act of 1995, imposing a unilateral economic embargo on the Islamic Republic. The only exceptions facilitated the transit of oil from the Caspian Sea.[1] It has been argued that President Clinton signed the act in an effort to stave off criticism from America's European allies about its hypocritical stance in advocating Iran's containment while channelling millions of dollars into its state coffers. Additionally, it has been maintained that Clinton succumbed to constant pressures by the belligerent, Republican-ruled Congress to bring about Iran's total isolation from the international community and thus to curtail its ability to acquire sophisticated weapons and to sponsor international terrorism. Probably his decision to impose sanctions on Iran when he did was a combination of both.

Some time later, in August 1996, the Iran-Libya Sanctions Act was passed. ILSA provided for sanctions against any firm, American or international, that invested more than $40 million in the energy industries of Iran and Libya. Although there were explicit references to Iran's nuclear programme, the act aimed primarily at curbing Iran's sponsorship of international terrorism, mainly owing to the US belief that 'Iran will not be able to produce sufficient plutonium to create a weapon until well into the next century, unless it receives significant foreign assistance.'[2] It seemed, however, that ILSA was in reality a means of discouraging foreign companies from supporting the so-called rogue states because it did not constitute a general trade embargo but concentrated solely on harming the energy sector, which accounts for the lion's share of Iranian state income. And at the same time, American and European energy companies were in effect being denied a big share of profitable international investments in Iran, which then had the world's fifth-largest proven crude oil reserves.

As a result, the act became the grounds for bitter confrontation between the European Union and the United States. The Europeans reacted collectively and tried to prevent the enactment of ILSA even before it was signed by President Clinton. As early as April 1996, the General Affairs and External Relations Council of the European Union noted that 'the draft US sanctions legislation concerning Iran and Libya . . . raises questions of extra-territoriality'. It urged its allies to avoid legislation that conflicted with international law and would harm EU interests and rights and invited 'the relevant EU experts to consider options for possible EU action' in case this was deemed necessary.[3] Immediately upon the signing of the act, the European Commission's vice president Sir Leon Brittan issued a statement in which he accused the United States of attempting to 'dictate the foreign policy of others' and warned that the European Union 'will act to defend its rights and interests if they are jeopardized by this legislation'.[4] The EU energy commissioner Christos Papoutsis expressed his deep concern about the 'big and serious problems' that the D'Amato Bill – as ILSA was frequently referred to, from Senator Alfonse D'Amato, who introduced it – would create for the European oil industry.[5] Some days later, the Irish presidency of the European Union, jointly with the Commission, made an official démarche to the US Department of State protesting against the signing of ILSA.[6] Already, the Council of the European Union had decided, in response to a similar US act,[7] on the measures to be taken in case of harmful effects on EU firms, among them a 'move to a WTO dispute settlement panel, changes in the procedures governing entry by representatives of US companies to EU Member States and the introduction of legislation within the EU to neutralize the extraterritorial effects of the US legislation'.[8] Over the following months, the European Union and the United States held a series of consultations under the World Trade Organization dispute settlement procedure, which brought the two partners to a common understanding in April 1997.[9]

As depicted above, ILSA was a source of tension in relations between the transatlantic allies. The Europeans reacted vigorously, for reasons that are evident, to the prospect of any sanctions involving the energy sector in Iran. The Treaty on European Union, which introduced the CFSP, had entered into force only in 1993. On the other hand, the 'critical dialogue' with Iran had been established in 1992. Finally, the period between 1989 and 1995 marked a peak in European imports of crude oil from Iran,[10] so it can be argued that the European Union intended to start investing in the Iranian oil industry, thus putting an end to American domination in the Iranian energy sector.

The case of Total and the developments after its resolution corroborate the above point. This case received much publicity and brought US–EU relations to a low ebb. In September 1997, the French oil company Total, along with Gazprom of Russia and the Malaysian oil company Petronas, signed a $2 billion contract with Iran's National Oil Company (NIOC).

This provided for the development of part of the South Pars natural gas and condensate field near Iran's maritime border with Qatar and for the extraction of 20 billion cubic metres of natural gas a year by 2001.[11] Before Total reached agreement with Iran, the Department of State investigated the contract and decided that it appeared to contravene ILSA. The United States warned that if Total went ahead with the contract, it might have to face sanctions from the Clinton administration.[12] Irritation on behalf of France and the European Union was evident in Sir Leon Brittan's statement of 30 September 1997. He urged the United States to 'reflect long and hard about the wisdom of taking any action against Total'.[13] The matter was finally resolved in the EU–US understanding of 11 April 1997: it was agreed that the United States would continue to use the presidential waiver authority against imposing sanctions on EU firms and that the European Union would refrain from establishing the WTO panel and would take under consideration nuclear proliferation concerns in its future political relations with Iran.[14] Nevertheless, the Europeans still set out a number of conditions, threatening to take the Americans to the WTO if any of them were not fulfilled, and pointed out that 'for the EU, it is axiomatic that infrastructural investment in the transport of oil and gas through Iran be carried out without impediment'.[15]

Arguably, Europe's dependence on oil imports and the prospect of large profits from contracts in Iran's energy sector were the reasons why it defied ILSA[16] (which, incidentally, was renewed in 2001). By contrast, America's need of Europe's support for its foreign policies led President Clinton to grant permanent waivers to European firms involved in Iran's oil and energy sector. In addition, ILSA provided safe ground for Europe to contest American hegemony because it was an economic issue, not a political one. In other words, it related to Europe's greatest strength: its economic might. Even though the will to forge political unification and a common foreign policy had started to become a reality, Europe was still at the beginning of this process, as the political failures in the Balkan conflicts in the early 1990s indicated. Thus a 'non-economic' direct encounter with the United States would most probably expose Europe's weaknesses in matters of critical political importance and thereby jeopardize its future as an international actor – something that European leaders could not afford. But a direct confrontation between the European Union and the United States on political issues would arise in the next decade, and Iran would have the leading role again.

Nuclear Weapons

Iran's nuclear programme started before 1979, when Shah Muhammad Reza Pahlavi signed agreements with the United States, Germany and France for the construction of nuclear power plants.[17] It continued after the Islamic revolution, but only recently have there been indications that the Islamic Republic might be developing a nuclear weapon. Iran is a signatory to the Nuclear Non-Proliferation Treaty (NPT) and has declared that its civilian nuclear facilities are open to IAEA (International Atomic Energy Agency) inspections. The IAEA had not detected any 'breach in the safeguards regime' in two visits to Iran's nuclear sites before March 1995,[18] and Iran did not object to the NPT's indefinite extension by the 1995 NPT review and extension conference.

Even so, US intelligence sources were alleging even then that Iran was trying to acquire nuclear weapons secretly and that its programme was based on 'indigenous training and development, the purchase of facilities ostensibly intended to support a civilian nuclear energy program (e.g. Russian reactors), and the illicit acquisition of controlled technologies and materials (possibly including fissile materials from the former Soviet Union) through an organized covert buying program'.[19] As a result, the American government had embarked by the early 1990s on the now infamous 'dual containment' policy that aimed at isolating Iran and prohibiting it from developing its nuclear programme.

'Dual containment' met with criticism even in the United States,[20] but nowhere more than in Europe. European criticism contained phrases such as 'empty rhetoric', 'incoherence' and an 'unhealthy obsession with Tehran'.[21] The Europeans were not really concerned about the possibility of direct military confrontation with Iran. On the contrary, they were enjoying fairly close economic ties with the Islamic Republic,[22] and they also shared a general sense of optimism about Iran's political direction after the accession to the presidency of Ali Akbar Hashemi Rafsanjani, widely considered to be a pragmatist. The recently created CFSP regarded human rights as a basic element of the European Union's foreign policy; and in view of Iran's rather weak record on human rights (Salman Rushdie, the Mykonos incident [see Chapter 4] etc.), the Union chose Iran as the testing ground for the CFSP by way of a 'critical dialogue' with the Iranians. Therefore, it sought to keep a channel of political communication open to the Iranian regime. It did of course remain concerned about Iran's nuclear programme, as a 1996 European Parliament report reveals. The report pointed out that Iran was allegedly trying to acquire a reactor 'by means of a nuclear deal with Russia', which was interpreted as an attempt 'to move closer to a nuclear weapons program';[23] and although a spokesman for the then Russian president Boris Yeltsin emphasized that 'the proliferation of nuclear and other types of weapons of mass destruction, . . . especially in countries adjacent and near to Russia, is considered a serious threat to Russia's security', implying perhaps that his country would halt exports of nuclear materials to Iran, the Russian foreign minister Yevgeny Primakov stated that his country 'would honor all contracts already signed'.[24]

The 'critical dialogue' was suspended briefly after the verdict of the German Federal Court implicated Iranian high officials in the Mykonos case. But after the accession of Mohammad Khatami to the presidency of the Islamic Republic in 1997, the European Union again entertained hopes for change in Iran. It took up the dialogue from where it had been left, renamed it 'comprehensive (or constructive) dialogue' and added human rights to the agenda, whose three other topics were the Middle East peace process, which Iran opposed vehemently, weapons of mass destruction and terrorism. Finally, on 17 June 2002, the Council of the European Union agreed on opening negotiations with the Islamic Republic on a trade and cooperation agreement.[25]

However, the United States claimed the vindication of its convictions when in December 2002 intelligence officials confirmed that Iran had failed to declare the construction of a heavy-water production plant at Arak and a gas-centrifuge plant at Natanz, which raised suspicions worldwide about the true nature of its nuclear programme.[26] Thus in 2003, after numerous press reports about Iran's nuclear activities, Javier Solana, the Union's CFSP High Representative, urged Tehran to make 'rapid progress in Iran's discussions with the IAEA' so that there will not be 'unwelcome effects on the EU's relations with Iran'.[27] In addition, the General Affairs and External Relations Council of the European Union, in its meeting of 16 June 2003, concluded that 'the nature of some aspects of Iran's [nuclear] program raises serious concerns, in particular as regards the closing of the nuclear fuel cycle, especially the uranium centrifuge, announced by President Khatami'. It called on Iran to cooperate fully with the IAEA and 'answer timely, fully and adequately all questions raised regarding its nuclear program'.[28] In effect, the European Union suspended negotiations for the trade and cooperation agreement in September 2003.[29]

Nevertheless, it continued its diplomatic efforts to convince Iran to freeze its nuclear activities, contrary to the United States, which adopted more aggressive tones in its rhetoric. Finally, representatives of Germany, France and the United Kingdom reached an agreement with the Iranian government on 15 November 2004 whereby Iran 'decided on a voluntary basis to continue and extend its suspension to include all enrichment related and reprocessing activities, and specifically: the manufacture and import of gas centrifuges; work to undertake any plutonium separation or to construct or operate any plutonium separation installation; and all tests or production at any uranium conversion installation'.[30] Subsequently, the European Union resumed negotiations for the trade and cooperation agreement, parallel to negotiations for a permanent solution to dangers posed by Iran's nuclear programme.[31] Yet, to this date the European Union has no contractual relations with Iran and the international community is still striving to convince Iran to give up its nuclear programme.

After these developments, a number of changes took place both in Iran and in the United States and the European Union. The introduced constitution of the European Union, intended to solidify its political unification and to establish a formalized and centralized administration, was rejected by France on 29 May 2005 and by the Netherlands on 1 June 2005, creating uncertainty about the future of the Union. Americans had already re-elected George W. Bush to a second term as president; and in his 2005 State of the Union Address, he singled out Iran as the world's primary state sponsor of terrorism and again accused it of attempting to acquire nuclear weapons. Then, Iran's presidential elections of 17 and 24 June 2005 brought to power Mahmoud Ahmadinejad, a religious conservative who was against promoting Iran–US relations and who had passionately defended Iran's nuclear programme in his campaign.

Finally, the International Atomic Energy Agency, following Europe's continuous attempts to resolve permanently the problems and suspicions arising from Iran's nuclear programme and its decision to resume uranium conversion activities at its facility in Isfahan on 1 August 2005,[32] adopted a resolution on 24 September 2005. This laid the ground for the referral of the Islamic Republic to the UN Security Council because, as mentioned in the resolution,

> the history of concealment of Iran's nuclear activities . . . the nature of these activities, issues brought to light in the course of the

Agency's verification of declarations made by Iran since September 2002 and the resulting absence of confidence that Iran's nuclear program is exclusively for peaceful purposes have given rise to questions that are within the competence of the Security Council, as the organ bearing the main responsibility for the maintenance of international peace and security.[33]

The resolution had the full backing of the European Union and the United States, but it did not include a definite date for the referral, thus allowing time for more diplomatic efforts towards a mutually acceptable solution.

Nevertheless, the congruence between the two sides was not so much a result of their concurrence on issues concerning Iran as an outcome of recent European discontent at the Islamic Republic's rejection of its limited economic and political incentives in exchange for the abandonment of its nuclear activities. It was perhaps an expression too of European concern for Iran's future after Ahmadinejad became president. A quick comparison of EU presidency declarations on the 2001 and the 2005 Iranian presidential elections shows that the Europeans expressed 'deep satisfaction at the commitment to democracy demonstrated by the Iranian people' at the 2001 elections, which saw Khatami, a representative of the clerical establishment widely acknowledged for his reformist ideas, re-elected to a second term of office. In 2005, the EU expressed regret that 'a very large majority of candidates, including many reformists and all the women, were excluded from the elections, making a genuine democratic choice difficult for the Iranian people', although Ahmadinejad was a layman, not a cleric.[34] Furthermore, in 2001 the European Union had issued a second declaration offering its 'warmest congratulations' to Khatami, but in 2005 Solana advised caution after the election of Ahmadinejad with regard to negotiations on Iran's nuclear programme.[35] Therefore, it seems that the European Union sided with the United States in adopting a harsh stance towards Iran at this time mostly as a form of retribution against Iran's stance towards European inducements and as a way to demonstrate its dissatisfaction with Iran's imminent political future.

Conclusion
In contrast to US administrations' 'dual containment' policy for dealing with Iran's proliferation of WMD and possible attempts to acquire nuclear

technology, the EU engaged Iran in a series of dialogues and negotiations, offering economic and political incentives in an effort to dissuade it from developing nuclear weapons. In other words, the United States decided to confront post-revolutionary Iran while the European Union chose to conciliate it. As a result, the European Union defied US legislation on Iran and confronted the Americans in prestigious international institutions.

Both approaches have been criticized for their failure to bring about the desired result. America's firm desire for a change of regime in Tehran in favour of one that would produce a democratic government (as defined by America itself) and restore diplomatic relations with the United States has yet to be realized. Between 1997 and 2005, when the reformist Khatami was president, there was some hope for 'democratic' changes in Iran, and a *rapprochement* with the United States started to emerge slowly. But the election of Ahmadinejad has shattered that prospect. On the other hand, the European engagement with and, in some cases, appeasement of Iran in order to mitigate its radical behaviour seems to have failed as well.

Although there is still no hard evidence that Iran is on the path of manufacturing nuclear weapons, much suspicion has accumulated. Shahram Chubin brilliantly presented in 1995 the motives, primarily psychological, for Iran's development of nuclear weapons. Iran's view then that the world was 'unjust and hostile towards it' has not changed significantly. Similarly, the complexity of the Iranian psyche, which reserves for itself an elevated position in the world and at the same time demonstrates a propensity for victimization and 'denial of responsibility', adds to the longing of Iranians to be reinstated to the status they deem to be appropriate in view of their glorious Islamic (and even pre-Islamic) past.[36] In addition, the fabrication of a constant outside threat to the Islamic Republic helps the Iranian government to avert public focus from an economy deficient because of mismanagement, corruption and personal rivalries. Chubin maintained that there was 'no debate about Iran "going nuclear" or about the place of nuclear weapons in current or future strategy'.[37] However, a brief inspection of the Iranian (and the international) press over the past two years would reveal that the debate about 'nuclear Iran' is thriving. Perhaps then, the 'ill-defined and fluid' intentions of Iran in 1995[38] have solidified and crystallized; and possibly this, along with the other reasons mentioned already, has driven the European Union to support a resolution that would subject Iran to UN sanctions.[39]

Nevertheless, this policy does not accept unilateral American punitive measures, for example ILSA. Instead, it allows for disciplinary actions on behalf of the international community and does not specify a definite starting point, thus allowing Iran to overturn it. Given the fragmentation prevalent in the European Union and the deficient and ineffective policies this fragmentation has caused, the European Union's unity on Iran and its opposition to US policy towards it might come as a surprise. Remarkably, this stance has continued more or less unaffected for the past 25 years. However, a passing examination of the political and economic environment in Europe in the 1990s shows that integration activities were favoured, and should have been expected. The Soviet bloc had disintegrated and new, smaller states had formed from some of its members. However, former Soviet satellite countries were striving to join the Western bloc. Also, the European economies were on a relatively good track, and Europe had just taken another firm step towards economic unification. There was in Europe an evident inclination for political unification and its reinstatement to 'great power' status. In addition, the ongoing disagreement within US administrations regarding policy towards the Islamic Republic only emboldened the European Union to pursue closer ties with Tehran and thus establish a stronghold in Iran.

Of course, the European Union is not yet on an equal footing with the United States. Nonetheless, it does strive to exert political influence outside its borders and seeks grounds to contest American hegemony. Iran seems to present the best opportunity for this not only because it is a staunch critic of US interventionism in the Middle East but also because it is a willing supplier of energy to Europe and welcomes European investment. Given also their common past, it comes as no surprise that the European Union has chosen Iran as its 'test subject' to experiment with the CFSP, to stand up to US interventionism and to safeguard its vested interests in the region. On the other hand, the United States recognizes that European support for its international policies, especially lately, is essential – not only because it faces criticism in many corners of the world but also because it has overstretched its resources and would certainly welcome a helping hand. For this reason, it seems willing to grant some 'political concessions' to the European Union, particularly in relation to those countries about which it understands that any aggressive approach and direct confrontation would produce everything *but* the desired results.

NOTES

1 Richard A. Falkenrath, 'The United States, Europe and Weapons of Mass Destruction', in Robert D. Blackwill and Michael Stürmer (eds), *Allies Divided: Transatlantic Policies for the Greater Middle East* (Cambridge, Mass., The MIT Press, 1997), p. 213.

2 Tony Capaccio, quoted in Ibid., p. 206.

3 General Affairs and External Relations Council, 1915th Council Meeting – General Affairs – Luxembourg, 22 April 1996 – President: Susanna Agnelli, Minister for Foreign Affairs of the Italian Republic, Nr. 6561/96 Presse: 98, Luxembourg, GAERC, 22 April 1996, p. 3.

4 European Commission, US President Signs Iran/Libya Law, DN: IP/96/776, Brussels, EU Institutions Press Releases, 6 August 1996, p. 1.

5 European Commission, D'Amato Bill–Commissioner C. Papoutsis' Reaction, DN: IP/96/778, Brussels, EU Institutions Press Releases, 6 August 1996, p. 1.

6 EC Presidency and European Commission, Irish Presidency and Commission Protested to the US Administration against the Iran/Libya Sanctions Act, DN: IP/96/793, Brussels, EU Institutions Press Releases, 9 August 1996, p. 1.

7 The Helms-Burton (or Libertad) Act on Cuba, passed on 12 March 1996.

8 General Affairs and External Relations Council, 1943rd Council Meeting – General Affairs – Brussels, 15/16 July 1996 – President: Dick Spring, Minister for Foreign Affairs of Ireland, Nr. 8913/96 Presse: 208, Brussels, GAERC, 16 July 1996, p. 14.

9 Subsequently the Council suspended the proceedings of the WTO dispute settlement panel, noting that they would be reopened if action were taken against EU companies or individuals under the D'Amato Act. CFSP Presidency, EU-US Helms-Burton, Nr. 7362/97 Presse: 110, Brussels, Council of the European Union, 18 April 1997, p. 1.

10 The data can be found in the Energy Pocketbooks of EUROSTAT for the relevant years.

11 Adam Tarock, 'Iran-Western Europe Relations on the Mend', *British Journal of Middle Eastern Studies*, vol. 26, 1999, p. 48.

12 It did point out, however, that it might waive sanctions under the national interest clause of the act or delay imposing them until consultations with France and the European Union took place. See Roy H. Ginsberg, *The European Union in International Politics: Baptism by Fire* (Lanham, Maryland: Rowman & Littlefield Publications), 2001, p. 242.

13 European Commission, Total Contract in Iran: Statement by Sir Leon Brittan, DN: IP/97/825, Brussels, EU Institutions Press Releases, 30 September 1997, p. 1.

14 European Commission, Understanding between the European Union and the United States on US extraterritorial legislation – 11 April 1997, in http://europa.eu.int/comm/external_relations/us/extraterritoriality/understanding_04_97.htm, accessed 1 March 2005.

15 General Affairs and External Relations Council, 2097th Council Meeting – General Affairs – Brussels, 25 May 1998 – President: Robin Cook, Secretary of State for Foreign and Commonwealth Affairs of the United Kingdom, Nr. 8687/98 Presse: 162, Brussels, GAERC, 25 May 1998, p. 9.

16 This also becomes evident from the developments that followed the agreement between the United States and the European Union. In 1999, Elf (France) and Agip (Italy) signed a deal with Iran to develop the Darood oil and gas field in the northern Gulf and boost the Iranian oil production to over 100,000 barrels a day. Later that year, Shell Exploration BV, an affiliate of Royal Dutch Shell, signed an $800 million deal with NIOC to develop the Soroush and Nowruz offshore fields (50 miles west of Kharg island), with the prospect of boosting production to 100,000 and 90,000 barrels a day respectively. Furthermore, in 2000 four European firms, Royal Dutch Shell, Agip, TotalFinaElf and Lasmo (UK) bid for a contract to upgrade production facilities for the oilfields of Ahwaz, Ab-e Teymour and Mansouri in the Bangestan reservoir in southern Iran. See 'European Oil Companies Defy US Over Iran Deal', BBC News, 1 March 1999; Geneive Abdo, 'US Inquiry Into Shell's Iran Deal', *The Guardian*, 15 November 1999; and 'European Oil Companies Submit Revised Bids for Bangestan Project', *Payvand*, 9 October 2000.

17 Oliver Thraenert, 'Iran, the Bomb, and the Future of the Nuclear Non-Proliferation Treaty', in Eugene Whitlock (ed.), *Iran and its Neighbors: Diverging Views on a Strategic Region* (Berlin: Stiftung Wissenschaft und Politik, 2003), p. 42.

18 Falkenrath, 'The United States, Europe and Weapons of Mass Destruction', p. 207.

19 Ibid., p. 206.

20 See Zbigniew Brzezinski, Brent Scowcroft and Richard Murphy, 'Differentiated Containment', *Foreign Affairs*, vol. 73, no. 3 (May/June 1997), pp. 20–30.

21 Falkenrath, 'The United States, Europe and Weapons of Mass Destruction', p. 213.

22 Iranian oil exports to Europe peaked in 1991. Italy, France and the United Kingdom were the major importers. In 1990, Germany imported 34.4 per cent of Iranian non-oil exports, and in 1992 the volume of German–Iranian trade relations was worth $6.8 billion. See Johannes Reissner, 'Europe and Iran: Critical Dialogue', in Richard N. Haass and Meghan L. O'Sullivan (eds), *Honey and Vinegar: Incentives, Sanctions and Foreign Policy* (Washington, DC: Brookings Institution Press, 2000), p. 36.

23 Martin Schulz, Report on the Communication from the Commission to the Council and the European Parliament: The Illicit Traffic in Radioactive Substances and Nuclear Materials, Strasbourg, European Parliament – Committee on Civil Liberties and Internal Affairs, 1 March 1996, p. 8.

24 Alain Gresh, 'No Option but Cooperation, Despite Conflicting Interests: The Iran Factor', *Le Monde Diplomatique*, June 1998, in http://mondediplo.com/1998/06/05gresh2, accessed 1 March 2005.

25 General Affairs and External Relations Council, 2437th Council Meeting – General Affairs – Luxembourg, 17 June 2002 – President: Josep Pique I Camps, Minister for Foreign Affairs of the Kingdom of Spain, Nr. 9717/02 Presse: 178, Luxembourg, GAERC, 17 June 2002, p. 16.

26 Michael Eisenstad, 'Dealing with Iran's Nuclear Program', in Whitlock (ed.), *Iran and its Neighbors*, p. 38.

27 'EU Envoy Warns Iran', BBC News, 30 August 2003, in http://news.bbc.co.uk/1/hi/ world/middleeast/3190319.stm, accessed 30 September 2003.

28 General Affairs and External Relations Council, 2518th Council Meeting – External Relations – Luxembourg, 16 June 2003 – President: Giorgos Papandreou, Minister for Foreign Affairs of the Hellenic Republic, Nr. 10369/03 Presse: 166, Luxembourg, GAERC, 16 June 2003, pp. 24–5.

29 General Affairs and External Relations Council, 2527th Council Meeting –
    External Relations – Brussels, 29 September 2003 – President: Franco Frattini,
    Minister for Foreign Affairs of the Italian Republic, Nr. 12294/03 Presse: 252,
    Brussels, GAERC, 29 September 2003, pp. 8–9.
30 Javier Solana, Statement by Javier Solana, EU High Representative for the CFSP,
    on the agreement on Iran's nuclear programme, S0304/04, Brussels, 15 November
    2004, p. 3.
31 See European Council Presidency, Brussels European Council (4/5 November
    2004) – Presidency Conclusions, Nr. 14292/04 CONCL 3, Brussels, Council of
    the European Union, 5 November 2004, pp. 9–10; General Affairs and External
    Relations Council, 2631st Council Meeting – External Relations – Brussels,
    13–14 December 2004 – President: Bernard Bot, Minister for Foreign Affairs of
    the Netherlands, Nr. 15461/04, Presse: 344, Brussels, 14 December 2004, p. 7;
    and European Council Presidency, Brussels European Council (16/17 December
    2004) – Presidency Conclusions, Nr. 16238/1/04, REV 1, CONCL 4, Brussels,
    Council of the European Union, 1 February 2005, p. 14.
32 See Permanent Mission of the Islamic Republic of Iran to the United Nations and
    Other International Organizations in Vienna, Verbal Note No. 350-1-17/928 to
    the IAEA Secretariat, Vienna, 1 August 2005, p. 5.
33 IAEA Board of Governors, Implementation of the NPT Safeguards Agreement
    in the Islamic Republic of Iran – Resolution adopted on 24 September 2005,
    GOV/2005/77, Vienna, IAEA, 24 September 2005, p. 2.
34 See Council of the European Union, Declaration by the Presidency on behalf
    of the European Union on the Presidential Election in Iran, Nr. 9399/01
    Presse: 227, Brussels, 11 June 2001, p. 1 and Council of the European Union,
    Declaration by the Presidency on behalf of the European Union on the
    Presidential Election in Iran, Nr. 10666/05 Presse: 173, Brussels, 28 June 2005,
    p. 1.
35 See Council of the European Union, Declaration by the Presidency on behalf
    of the European Union Following the Swearing in of the President of Iran,
    Nr. 11219/01 Presse: 304, Brussels, 10 August 2001, p. 1 and Secretary
    General/High Representative for CFSP, Comments by EU HR Javier Solana on
    the Final Results of the Iranian Presidential Elections, Nr. S236/05, Brussels, 27
    June 2005, p. 1.
36 Shahram Chubin, 'Does Iran Want Nuclear Weapons?', *Survival*, vol. 37, no. 1
    (Spring 1995), pp. 87–8.
37 Ibid., p. 86.
38 Idem.
39 Security Council Resolution 1737 (2006) that called on all States to prevent
    Iran from acquiring 'items, materials, equipment, goods and technology which
    could contribute to Iran's enrichment-related, reprocessing or heavy water-related
    activities, or to the development of nuclear weapon delivery systems'.

6

Iran–United Kingdom Relations since the Revolution: Opening Doors

Christopher Rundle

Tehran zibast. Khoda zibai-ra dust darad. (Tehran is beautiful. God loves beauty.) These words on a sign caught my eye one day as I was travelling along an expressway in Tehran. Signs by the side of the road can be indicative of the mood of the times, and that particular one belonged to the time when Gholamhossein Karbaschi was mayor of Tehran. Having made Isfahan green, he was now doing the same for Tehran: trees were being planted on hillsides, parks were being revitalized and pavements were being cleared of makeshift stalls. Thanks to his and later efforts, visitors to Tehran these days talk of its public spaces being orderly and beautiful.

In less green times, shortly after the revolution, other words used to appear frequently on the walls of the British embassy in Ferdowsi Avenue. In translation, they were:

America is worse then Britain.
Britain is worse than America.
The Soviet Union is worse than both.

These words would stay on the walls for quite a time: we were short-staffed and had no First Secretary Anti-graffiti.

I shall come to their significance in a moment. But I remember that a time came when the authorities decided to ban the public from writing slogans on other people's walls. Ali Akbar Nateq Nouri, at one time Minister of the Interior and later Speaker of the Majlis, was asked at a press conference the reason for this. His reply was that the Islamic Republic had developed official machinery for taking decisions on foreign policy and individuals should not interfere by daubing their own thoughts on walls. At the centre of the policy machinery, he said, was the Supreme National Security Council.

This body was thus considered years ago to be the coordinating point for Iran's foreign policy, and by all accounts it remains so. The question nevertheless used to be asked, and is still relevant today, to what extent was and is Iran's foreign and security policy coordinated? It was posed again in the summer of 2004 when three British patrol boats being used to train the Iraqi river patrol service were intercepted by Iranian forces in the Shatt al-Arab, the waterway separating Iran and Iraq. Relations between Iran and Britain at the time were rather tense – demonstrations had taken place outside the British embassy in Tehran in protest at the occupation of Iraq – and there were fears in some quarters that the Revolutionary Guards who intercepted the patrol boats might be out of control. But the matter was settled quite speedily once it had been referred to the centre, to the extent that the military personnel in the boats were released within days although the boats remained in Iranian hands.

Perhaps people in the West should not be too worried. And if there is a theme in this chapter, it is that relations between our two countries are strong enough now not to be blown off course by incidents such as these. I might add too that in talking about the past, my intention is not to rake over old coals but to show how much improvement in relations there has been since the early days of the revolution. Although one cannot talk about relations now actually being good, they are at least stable, and there is more understanding than before on both sides.

So what about the slogan about Britain being worse than America and vice versa and the Soviet Union being worse than both? This was a quotation from a speech made by Ayatollah Khomeini in 1964, shortly before he went into exile.[1] And it was consistent with one of the main slogans of the revolution: 'Neither East nor West, an Islamic Republic'.[2] Iran after the Islamic revolution was looking for a third way – between the two superpowers, between capitalism and communism. The country to which it was most hostile was, for obvious reasons, the United States, and the Islamic Republic was opposed to the Soviet Union because of its atheistic philosophy and its support for Marxist groups. But the point to note here is that Britain, although far from being a superpower, was put in the same category as those two. This was because of our past involvement and interference in Iran's affairs and a lingering suspicion as to what we might be up to now. Among other things, the memory of the British role in the CIA-led coup that overthrew the nationalist government of Muhammad Musaddiq in 1953 and restored the Shah to his throne was still fresh in Iranian minds.

Recently, I came across some cuttings from the Tehran press that I had kept since the early 1980s.[3] They contained a series of articles on the history of British relations with Iran, detailing among other things the concessions and privileges accorded by the Qajar dynasty in the nineteenth century. One of them spoke of the British embassy acting then in a domineering manner, and went so far as to claim that the British ambassador had the habit of giving orders to the Shah. This chimed exactly with a speech that I remember Ayatollah Khomeini making some years after the revolution in which he declared that the days when the British ambassador would give orders to Iran's rulers had gone.

Because of all the history, conspiracy theories about Britain abounded after the revolution. Foremost among them was a preposterous but quite widely held belief that it had instigated the revolution itself out of jealousy for the position that the United States had built up with the Shah. Another was that the British embassy had for decades been in collusion with the Shia clergy, although the sum of our contacts seems actually to have been the annual meeting over a cup of tea between the ambassador and Imam Jomeh of Tehran, who was an appointee of the Pahlavi court. (More recently, a story has been doing the rounds of a British diplomat asking an Iranian in the street when he thought the regime might change. 'Well, how should I know? It is up to you British, isn't it?') However wide of the mark such tales of intrigue might be, they signified that after the revolution our relations were extremely sensitive.

Because of these sensitivities, the United Kingdom became after the revolution what one might call a 'least-favoured nation'. This was evident in, among other things, the terms of trade. In the 1970s, Iran had been the United Kingdom's largest market in the Middle East. But after the revolution, that position, and our share of the Iranian market, fell away sharply. From time to time, there were rumours of black lists in the Iranian ministries either banning trade with us or advocating the purchase of British goods last. But the news was not all bad. For example, despite various problems, the assembly of the Paykan automobile continued. Based on the Hillman Hunter, it had established itself since 1967 as the most common car and taxi on Tehran's streets. (I remember that on my first visit to Iran, in that very year, I imported a Hillman Hunter for my own use, to the astonishment of numerous Iranians who could not believe that such a car had been made in Britain.) The Paykan ended production only in 2005, by then an outdated workhorse but also a symbol of lasting cooperation.

On the diplomatic front, the British embassy held on during the time of the provisional government under Mehdi Bazargan in 1979 with a reduced staff. There was some optimism in the summer that things might be returning to a semblance of normality. Working in Iran for several months, I was able to travel to the Caspian without incident and to attend occasions such as the inauguration of the Assembly of Experts, the body that debated the Islamic Republic's new constitution. The Americans were even thinking of appointing a new ambassador.[4] But instead, the occupation of the American embassy in November led to an international crisis, and in April 1980 the British ambassador, Sir John Graham, was withdrawn. It was to be nearly 20 years before a new one was appointed.

Things reached an almost all-time low in the autumn of 1980, when we closed the embassy and placed it under Swedish protection. It was inevitably rumoured that we had done this in solidarity with the United States. But the truth of the matter was that there had been demonstrations outside the embassy and that the Iranian foreign minister, no less, had warned us that the authorities could not guarantee its safety. When that foreign minister, the ill-starred Sadeq Qotbzadeh, was removed, we decided, because of the volatility of Iranian politics at the time, not to reveal to his successor the identity of the person who had given us the warning. That could only have added to Iranian suspicion about our behaviour.

Unfortunately, the Iranian embassy in London turned out to be at greater risk than ours in Tehran.[5] In April 1980, it was taken over by armed Arabs from Iran demanding autonomy for Khuzestan, which they referred to as Arabistan. They were trained and supported by Iraq, which later that year was to give 'liberation' of the area as one of its reasons for invading Iran. During the resulting siege and, finally, the dramatic liberation operation by the Special Air Service, two members of the embassy staff were shot dead by the hostage-takers and all but one of the gunmen were killed. In addition, the chargé d'affaires, Dr Ali Afrouz, was injured at the beginning of the episode while trying to escape. Although the Iranian authorities thanked Britain officially for the way the occupation was ended, the incident cast a shadow over our relations, and it was followed by protracted negotiations concerning compensation for damage done to the embassy building during the rescue.

The French poet Alfred de Musset once wrote a play with the title *Il faut qu'une porte soit ouverte ou fermée* [A Door must be either Open or Shut]. Despite Britain's attempts to prize the door open, the embassy remained officially closed for years. The Iranians' attitude was, perhaps understandably, that they wanted to keep us in our place. We once learnt that there was about to be a meeting of deputy ministers of the Ministry of Foreign Affairs to discuss the matter and that at least one of them was in favour of us reopening. But he was overruled; one of the other deputy ministers was known to be vehemently anti-British, and the hardliners won the day.

A number of British diplomats were nevertheless allowed to work in the British embassy building – in what was called the British Interests Section, with the Swedish flag flying outside – and I happened to be one of them. I had worked in the embassy a couple of times after the revolution, but began a full posting only in January 1981, by chance leaving London for Tehran on 20 January, the day the American hostages were freed. Although we had had indications that their ordeal might be coming to an end, I was not aware that their release would happen that day. The news of it gave a good feeling.[6]

When I got to Tehran, one of my tasks was to tell the Iranian authorities that we had 'no quarrel with the Iranian revolution'. This translated poorly into Persian, and seemed a rather strange thing to say as our interests had clearly been damaged and we disagreed with Iran on a number of issues, including stability in the Persian Gulf. Eventually, we changed the language and said, truthfully, that we accepted the revolution and wanted to develop a normal relationship. But the opportunity to do this came only after long years of deadlock, in 1988, when the Iran–Iraq war ended and there was a reduction in tension. Leading Iranian figures, including the speaker of the Majlis, Akbar Hashemi Rafsanjani, were saying openly by then that Iran had made too many enemies.

Iran then began to conduct what it called an 'open-door' policy towards all countries with the exception of Israel, the United States and South Africa, this last being considered a racist state.[7] The Iranians were eager to get closer to European countries in particular, as well as the

Arab states, most of which had favoured Iraq during the war. One result of the change in atmosphere was that the British embassy was reopened towards the end of 1988 after negotiations that took place largely in Geneva. It says something for the priorities of the British public that the London newspapers paid more attention to the Afghan hound, a *tazi*, which accompanied Gordon Pirie, the first officer to leave for Tehran, than to his mission itself. (The dog looked undernourished, but I was later assured that it was just lean and fit, as a hunting dog should be.)

More importantly, it seemed then that diplomatic relations might at last be returning to an even keel. The rival claims for compensation – for the damage to the Iranian embassy in 1980 and, from the British side, for the damage done to the British embassy by a mob at the time of the revolution – had already been settled in the summer of 1988, and in general it looked as though pragmatic voices in Tehran were in the ascendant. The joint announcement that full diplomatic representation would be resumed was accompanied by a statement that this would be based on reciprocity, mutual respect and non-interference in each other's affairs.

In those days, however, something always seemed to happen to throw matters off course. On this occasion, it was the publication in London of Salman Rushdie's book *The Satanic Verses* and the Iranian reaction to it.[8] The book was published in September 1988. Shortly afterwards, it was banned in a number of Muslim countries, and demonstrations were mounted against it in several of them. There were also demonstrations in Britain, with copies of the book being burnt in public in Bradford. People in Iran took very little notice at first, but in February 1989 the controversy deepened dramatically. After riots in Pakistan, in which more than five people lost their life, Ayatollah Khomeini made a pronouncement on the subject in which he effectively condemned Rushdie to death.[9]

This set Iran and the United Kingdom on a collision course. Pragmatic voices in both countries immediately tried to find a way out. The British foreign secretary Sir Geoffrey Howe said publicly that he understood that the book had been found deeply offensive by people of the Muslim faith. Rushdie himself issued a carefully worded statement of regret. Rafsanjani said that too much of a hullabaloo should not be made in response to the expression of opinion by an Islamic authority, as if to say that on this occasion Khomeini's word was not law. But there was no question of the British government issuing an apology or banning the book. And on the Iranian side, there was no prospect of repealing the edict, which became known in the West as a fatwa, although many authorities in Iran considered it to be a *hokm* and therefore to have the force of a decree. In March 1989, Iran broke diplomatic relations with Britain over the affair. After all those years of waiting, the first attempt at reopening the British embassy had lasted no more than three months.

Iraq's invasion of Kuwait in August 1990 gave the United Kingdom and Iran an incentive to resume diplomatic relations in the next month. From the British perspective, it was important to be able to discuss the Kuwait crisis with Iran, a regional power and an immediate neighbour of Iraq. There were also a number of other sensitive issues to be resolved. One was the problem of British hostages held by the Iranian-backed Hezbollah in Lebanon. Another was the fate of Roger Cooper, a British journalist and businessman employed by the American firm McDermott International, a leading marine construction company.[10] He had been visiting Iran from Dubai on business when he was arrested and imprisoned on a charge of spying. Although there was a body of opinion in the United Kingdom against improving relations as long as the Rushdie problem remained unresolved, it was thought more advantageous to conduct a proper dialogue on matters, including the removal of the threat to Rushdie's life.

What did Iran's foreign policy-makers want at this stage – after the Iran–Iraq war had ended and now that Iraq had invaded Kuwait? I would suggest four interlinked objectives. First, it sought to create an international atmosphere favourable to the survival of the regime. Perhaps its greatest achievement so far was to have survived given the forces that had at one time or another been ranged against it: Iraq, much of the rest of the Arab world, the United States and various internal opponents.[11] An improved security environment was now essential. The neutralization of the threat from Iraq would be an important part of that.

Second, Iran wanted international respectability. It had been branded a rogue state as a result of the American hostage crisis and had been cold-shouldered and placed under pressure by the international community during the war with Iraq, and now was the time for it to seek reintegration into the international community.

Third, and linked to that, Iran wanted fair and equal treatment. Thus relations with Western countries in particular should be on a reciprocal basis. (In one respect at least, the United Kingdom had allowed things to be weighted in Iran's advantage. While British diplomats functioned for years as the British Interests Section of the Swedish embassy, Iran had kept its embassy in place in London, under a chargé d'affaires, from the time of the revolution until Iran itself broke relations in 1989.)

Fourth, Iran wished to expand its economic and commercial relations. The revolution and years of war had badly scarred its economy, and Iran was now entering a phase of reconstruction. Existing oilfields needed to be restored to full production and new ones to be established. Shortages of consumer goods had to be alleviated by means of increased imports, and foreign investment in industrial projects needed to be encouraged. In addition, financial and technical assistance were to be sought.

Improved relations with the United Kingdom could contribute to all these goals. (The expertise of British companies in the oil and gas industries is thought to have weighed particularly heavily with the Iranian side.) Normalization of relations with the United Kingdom may also have been seen by some as a stepping stone to relations with the United States: although Iran could survive without America, the hostile nature of the relationship was harming it both politically and economically. Logic demanded that in the long term a way should be found to end the confrontation.

At the same time, Iran had a number of bones to pick with the British government, including the presence of members of the Mojahedin-e Khalq organization in the United Kingdom, the question of *The Satanic Verses* and, as Iran saw it, British double standards vis-à-vis Iran, on the one hand, and the Gulf monarchies, on the other. There was a feeling too that despite its formal position of impartiality during the Iran–Iraq conflict, Britain had favoured the Iraqi side.

Nevertheless, Iran–UK relations gradually improved during the early 1990s. British aid was welcomed when a major earthquake hit north-western Iran in June 1990, several months before diplomatic relations resumed. During 1991, the remaining British hostages in Lebanon, John McCarthy, Jackie Mann and Terry Waite, were all released. In that year, an Iranian, Mehrdad Kowkabi, who had been charged with conspiracy to cause arson in bookshops selling *The Satanic Verses,* was returned to Iran after a judge at the Old Bailey (the Central Criminal Court) in London had stopped his trial. Kowkabi's case had been given a high profile in Iran and had been linked in some people's minds with the continued imprisonment of Roger Cooper. Not long after Kowkabi's release, Cooper himself was released and flew back to London. On the commercial side, British exports began to rise again, and record numbers of British exhibitors took part in the annual international trade fair in Tehran in 1992. On the diplomatic side, relations became more businesslike even though the Rushdie affair held back agreement to exchange ambassadors, and the tit-for-tat expulsions of diplomats of the 1980s continued.

These positive developments in Iran–UK relations contributed to the decision by the European Community in December 1992 to embark on a 'critical dialogue' with Iran. Its aim was to encourage changes in Iranian behaviour on matters such as human rights and support for terrorism and to move towards constructive cooperation. Besides criticism, there would be incentives tied to specific demands. There were often significant differences of view among the European partners about the best approach to adopt towards Iran on particular issues – the European Community/Union's Common Foreign and Security Policy was not launched until 1993. But on most occasions, a measure of agreement was reached, and the United Kingdom benefited from the degree of European solidarity achieved. After various ups and downs over the next years, in 1998 the European Union under the British presidency began a new, more comprehensive dialogue with Iran that addressed matters of mutual interest.

The election of Muhammad Khatami as the president of Iran in May 1997, which took many people by surprise, paved the way for a more constructive dialogue between Iran and Britain as well as the EU states generally. Khatami spoke of the need to have relations with all countries that respected Iran's independence, dignity and national interests, and talked the language of opening doors rather than closing them. In September 1998, a 'diplomatic resolution' of the Rushdie problem was found at last. The Iranian government dissociated itself from Ayatollah Khomeini's edict by stating that it would take no action to threaten the life of the author of *The Satanic Verses* and would not encourage or assist anybody to do so. The British government said that it understood and regretted the offence that the book had caused to Muslims in Iran and elsewhere in the world.

At the same time, the British and Iranian foreign ministers, who were meeting quietly at the UN General Assembly in New York, agreed that diplomatic relations should be upgraded to ambassadorial level and expressed the hope that a more constructive relationship might now be possible.[12] This agreement was followed by increased cooperation in a number of fields: trade, education, culture, assistance for the large number of Afghan and Iraqi refugees in Iran and support for Iran's efforts to curb drug trafficking from Afghanistan. (In 2004, there were still an estimated one million refugees in Iran. Since the fall of the Taliban, the opium crop in Afghanistan has increased and counter-narcotics operations have become even more important. Iran is a key route for drugs on the way to European markets.) Assistance was also given with clearing landmines left from the Iran–Iraq war. In December 2003, when an earthquake struck the historic town of Bam, a UNESCO World Heritage Site situated between Kerman and Zahedan in south-eastern Iran, the United Kingdom sent a search-and-rescue team and other assistance.

In trade, a minor landmark was reached in December 2002 when the Export Credits Guarantee Department provided the first full cover for an Iranian project for 20 years – for a petrochemical project at Bandar Imam Khomeini, the former Bandar Shahpur. Although still not nearly back to pre-revolutionary levels, British exports to Iran continued to grow, and a number of trade missions were mounted in both directions. The Lord Mayor of London was among those who visited Tehran promoting the British capital's financial services and industries.

On the diplomatic front, Kamal Kharrazi, Iran's foreign minister, visited London in January 2000 and met the prime minister. Jack Straw, his British counterpart, returned his visit in September 2001. Although relations became strained in February 2002 when Iran rejected the United Kingdom's nominee as its next ambassador to Iran, London did not allow this to push things completely off course, and a different appointment was made later in the year.[13] Relations have since proceeded quite smoothly. However, an indication of continued sensitivity was provided during the visit to Bam by the Prince of Wales in February 2004. He was travelling in his capacity as the president of the British Red Cross, and was not on an official visit, but some Iranians chose to see this first visit to their country by a member of the British royal family since the revolution as British legitimation of the then re-emerging hard-line trend in Iranian politics.

In response to President Khatami's advocacy of a 'dialogue among civilizations',[14] itself a response in part to Huntington's theory of a 'clash of civilizations', the United Kingdom has supported an interfaith dialogue between British and Iranian academics and faith leaders since 2000. I attended one such meeting in Tehran in the spring of 2002. The British side was represented by Muslims as well as Christians; on the Iranian side there were Armenians, other Christians, Zoroastrians and Jews as well as Muslims. The Iranian team was led by a prominent representative of the ulema, Ayatollah Mohammadi Araghi. He was eager to stress that the Koran itself had invited Muslims to have a dialogue with those of other faiths; he considered it as an important way to create mutual understanding. A potential problem, he said, was how to reconcile the idea of the truth of a particular religion with the religious diversity that existed in the world, but Shia theologians were not of the opinion that other religions did not possess truth. A striking part of the meeting was a confident presentation by an Armenian lady. She outlined the contribution that the Armenian community was making to Iranian cultural and commercial life and explained the status of its religion in Iran, a country that, she said, had long been a multicultural society. Needless to say, when I raised the question of the Bahais in the general discussion, the Iranian response was the standard one: they represented a political group rather than a religion. The meeting was nevertheless something of a landmark: it was the first time I had been able to have a discussion with members of the Shia clergy inside Iran.

For some years now, the British government's policy towards Iran has been one of 'constructive engagement', in marked contrast to the isolationist stance of the United States. The American administration has of course inherited a different set of circumstances, going back to the revolution itself and the hostage crisis. Also, it has a somewhat different world view. British policy has not been easy to maintain in the face of those who think either that Iran is about to implode or that George W. Bush was near the mark when he talked about an 'axis of evil'. But despite this, British political contacts with Iran have been growing impressively, with ministerial visits in both directions and visits by parliamentary delegations. Jack Straw, as foreign secretary, visited Iran no fewer than four times, most recently in October 2003. However, British ministers have said that relations with Iran can develop only if it takes action to address general political concerns, including about human rights,[15] and particularly the inadequacy of judicial proceedings, restrictions on freedom of expression and discriminatory treatment of religious minorities.

The United Kingdom has long seen Iran as an important country in a strategic area of the world; and in the past few years, it has assumed increased international importance as well as greater significance for Britain's own national interests. In economic terms, Iran is not only oil-rich but increasingly sought after for gas supplies: it has the second largest reserves of natural gas in the world after Russia.[16]

Sandwiched between Iraq and Afghanistan, the two countries whose regimes have been changed by coalition action and which now exist uneasily between instability and democracy, Iran has more immediate relevance to Britain's political and security interests: better surely to have it as an ally, or at least a neutral, than a spoiler. The fall of the Taliban in 2001 removed a threat to Iran itself, and since then Iran has been committed to the reconstruction of Afghanistan. It is implementing aid projects, notably in the Herat area, and providing Afghanistan with large quantities of oil. Recently, it provided equipment for Bamiyan airport in the centre of the country. On Iraq, although it was critical of the coalition's military action, Iran took a neutral stance during the major hostilities. Since then, it has been broadly supportive of efforts to promote the stability of the Iraqi state (while opposing the foreign military presence) because it does not desire chaos on its borders, the formation of a Kurdish republic or the complete disintegration of the country. A landmark was the visit of the Iraqi prime minister to Iran in July 2005. Border security and anti-terrorism measures were among subjects discussed, as well as economic relations.

In the global 'war against terrorism', Iran has an important position in two respects. The first, noted above, through which it has played a broadly positive role, is its physical position adjacent not only to Iraq but also to Afghanistan and Pakistan, the other post-9/11 front-line states in this campaign. The second, negative, consideration is the material and political support it has given to Hezbollah and radical Palestinian groups such as Hamas which have sought to undermine the Middle East peace process. Iran has stated that it would not reject a two-state solution provided that it was acceptable to both the Israelis and the Palestinians, but its support for militant groups is still a matter of concern for the United Kingdom and the European Union.

In addition to the above concerns has been another matter of global importance, nuclear non-proliferation. Britain has been, with France and Germany, one of the European trio negotiating with Iran on the issue and seeking to avoid international confrontation. Much hangs on the future of these talks. One of the United Kingdom's first moves after the election of Mahmoud Ahmadinejad as president in June 2005 was to express the hope that Iran would take early steps to address international concerns about its nuclear programme.

Were it not for non-proliferation and the 'war against terrorism' – and the complicating factor of the Bush administration's attitude towards Iran's internal politics – relations between the United Kingdom and Iran would undoubtedly have advanced further than they have. As it is, one measure of success in developing the relationship has been that British exports to Iran rose from some £300 million in 2000 to £444 million in 2004, and these figures would be much higher if re-exports from places such as Dubai were included. Nevertheless, the United Kingdom's exports have lagged behind those of its main European competitors, Germany, Italy and France, and it should not be thought that commercial considerations are uppermost in the British mind when dealing with Iran. In the current international climate, issues of global security come higher up the list.

From Iran's perspective, I would judge that Britain is of particular importance because of its permanent membership of the UN Security Council, its active presence in the European Union, its military power and its closeness to the United States, although as America's foremost ally Britain is considered to be too close. (When Iran and the United States get down to serious talking, they will not be looking for intermediaries: Iran will want to talk direct, and knows that the United Kingdom has limited influence in Washington.) Iran's desire to have a steady relationship with the United Kingdom was evident in a statement by its foreign ministry in June 2003 in which it justified a visit by Jack Straw shortly after the British prime minister had issued a statement in support of students demonstrating in Iran. The foreign ministry said that Straw's visit was necessary because 'closing the doors would solve nothing' and because it would not be appropriate to convey Iran's viewpoints and positions to its European friends through the media.[17] So these days, in marked contrast to the 1980s, conscious efforts are being made to keep doors open.

Parallel with the improvement in Iran–UK political relations, there has been a remarkable increase in cultural ties. In London these days, one can go to Iranian films, concerts of Iranian music, recitals of Persian poetry, exhibitions by Iranian artists and any number of lectures on subjects ranging from carpet design to the role of *ta'azieh* (plays concerning the martyrdom of Imam Hossein) in Iranian life. Particularly noteworthy was a London-wide programme of events in 2005 celebrating the achievements of the film-maker, photographer and artist Abbas Kiarostami. Both the National Film Theatre and the Institute of Contemporary Arts – the latter is famed as being at the cutting edge of modern culture – hosted his works. In Oxford, there has been a conference on contemporary Iranian art, organized in association with the Tehran Museum of Contemporary Art. Intrigued perhaps by its very complexity, the promoters described the art under discussion as 'engaged in a search for authenticity and at the same time struggling to create its own hybridity'.

In Iran too, cultural ties are on the increase. The British Council reopened an office in Tehran in 2001. Its initial focus was on strengthening educational cooperation and English-language teaching, but more recently it has broadened its activities and fostered cultural exchanges and also helped to develop scientific and technological links. Among the events that it has arranged was an exhibition of contemporary British sculpture at the Tehran Museum of Contemporary Art in 2004, the first exhibition of British art or sculpture to be seen in Iran since the revolution. On display were works by sculptors ranging from Henry Moore to Gilbert and George. The British Institute of Persian Studies (BIPS) has likewise seen a growth in its activities in Iran, with increased cooperation between British and Iranian archaeologists. Following the earthquake at Bam, BIPS offered expert assistance to the Iranian Cultural Heritage Organization.[18] The quality, and sheer weight, of its annual journal *Iran* attests to the abiding interest of British scholars in Persian culture in its widest sense.

To sum up, Iran and the United Kingdom have a number of mutual concerns and interests, and there is a firmer foundation for bilateral relations now than at any time since the revolution. Both sides have had to work hard to achieve this. Disagreements will continue to exist, and we still need better mutual understanding. I sense that there are frustrations on both sides. Iran may well think that its numerous acts of cooperation with Western powers over the years, and most recently over Afghanistan and Iraq, have received an inadequate payback. Britain may feel caught in the middle between an Iran that is cynical about the international system and a United States that seeks to control the system. (Which is considered the devil and which the deep blue sea may depend on where one is sitting.) Putting effort into the relationship will continue to be important for both sides. There is always the possibility that it may be blown off course by unforeseen events. But provided Tehran and London maintain a measured approach, the prospects for long-term improvement in their relationship are good. From the United Kingdom's perspective, Iran is high up on the list of foreign policy priorities.[19]

NOTES

1 See Hamid Algar, *Islam and Revolution: Writings and Declarations: Imam Khomeini* (London: KPI, 1985), p. 185 and Baqer Moin, *Khomeini: Life of the Ayatollah* (London, I.B. Tauris, 1999), p. 125.

2 For a discussion of the slogan 'Neither East nor West' see R.K. Ramazani, *Revolutionary Iran* (Baltimore and London: Johns Hopkins University Press, 1986), pp. 19–31.

3 *Jomhuriye Eslami*, 5 November 1984.

4 The last American ambassador, William Sullivan, left Iran in April 1979.

5 There is an account of the embassy siege in Chris Cramer and Jim Harris, *Hostage* (London: J. Clare, 1982).

6 For an account of subsequent events in Iran–UK relations, see Christopher Rundle, *From Colwyn Bay to Kabul* (Stanhope: The Memoir Club, 2004), pp. 120–59.

7 An 'open-door' policy had been announced earlier. See the speech by Ayatollah Seyyed Ali Khamenei, then President of the Islamic Republic, to a gathering of Iranian ambassadors as reported by IRNA news agency, 6 August 1988.

8 Salman Rushdie, *The Satanic Verses* (London: Viking, 1988).

9 See Moin, *Khomeini*, pp. 282–4 and Rundle, *From Colwyn Bay to Kabul*, pp. 146–50.

10 See Roger Cooper, *Death Plus Ten Years* (London: HarperCollins, 1993).

11 Saudi Arabia and Kuwait bankrolled the Iraqi war effort. Egypt took a pro-Iraqi stance. Oman attempted to act as a mediator between Iran and Iraq. Only Syria sided with Iran.

12 Statements by the Iranian and British foreign ministers in New York, 24 September 1998.

13 After the nomination of David Reddaway had been rejected in February 2002, the UK decided to function for a time at chargé d'affaires level and to restrict access for the Iranian ambassador in London. The next British ambassador, Richard Dalton, took up his post in December 2002.

14 For a discussion of Khatami's concept of a 'dialogue among civilizations', see Ali M. Ansari, *Iran, Islam and Democracy* (London: The Royal Institute of International Affairs, 2000), pp. 129–40.

15 Statement by Baroness Symons, House of Lords, 3 December 2004.

16 Iran was among possible key future producers of natural gas identified by the British government when it embarked on a new energy strategy in October 2004. The United Kingdom is expected to be importing 50 per cent of its gas requirements by 2010.

17 Statement by the Iranian foreign ministry spokesman Hamid-Reza Asefi, IRNA news agency, 30 June 2003.
18 The task of rebuilding the ancient citadel at Bam will take many years. The immediate task for BIPS was to collect photographic and historical evidence on behalf of the Bam Restoration Office in order to help with decisions on restoration.
19 Article by John Sawers, Director General at the Foreign and Commonwealth Office, in the FCO's publication *Connect,* Issue 19, April/May 2006, p. 4.

7

Diplomatic Relations Between Iran and the United Kingdom in the Early Reform Period, 1997–2000

Michael Axworthy

This chapter aims to give an overview of diplomatic relations between Iran and Britain from the election of President Khatami in 1997 to the summer of 2000 from the perspective of someone involved in the formulation of British policy at that time.[1] In addition to surveying the essential facts, it offers some analysis of motives and intentions, and tries to draw out some points about the effects of internal political developments and of Iran's previous international isolation. The chapter examines the improvement in those relations after the election of Khatami, particularly after statements by the two governments addressing the Rushdie problem in September 1998. It considers the range of policy matters discussed between the two countries, giving due weight to the influence of EU policy. It discusses the British perception of Iranian intentions and policy constraints and addresses some of the problems that arose between the two sides over this period as well as their joint achievements.

Christopher Rundle in Chapter 6 has contributed an account of the ups and downs in the relationship between the United Kingdom and Iran since the revolution of 1979, and I shall not repeat that background. Clearly, it was a troubled story, reflecting the difficulties, misunderstandings and crises that arose between the governments of the two countries in earlier times, in whose history the dates 1805–12, 1906 and 1953 are significant. When President Khatami took office in May 1997, Britain and Iran had representatives in each others' countries, but only at a low level. Just one month earlier, EU heads of mission had left Tehran in protest after a German court implicated the Iranian government in the bombing in Berlin in 1992 of the Mykonos restaurant (in which four

Iranian Kurdish dissidents died), and the United Kingdom had agreed with the suspension of previous contacts by the European Union that had been maintained since 1992 under the 'critical dialogue'.

The fatwa against Salman Rushdie had been an additional, major obstacle to the improvement of relations between the United Kingdom and Iran since 1989. But it soon became clear to the British side that the election of President Khatami could mark a significant change, and its perception was that some on the Iranian side saw the election of a Labour government in the United Kingdom as an opportunity too for an attempt to bridge the gap between the two countries.

The British chargé d'affaires Nick Browne returned to Tehran in November 1997, and over the next months it emerged from various meetings that there could be scope for resolving the Rushdie problem. Before the formation of the Khatami government, the Iranians had told us on various occasions that they had no intention of sending commandos to assassinate Rushdie. The British government's view was that these indications were not reassuring enough: they left open other possibilities, such as that the Iranian government might send instead a group of sailors or interior decorators. But when the foreign secretary Robin Cook met his counterpart Dr Kamal Kharrazi in the margins of the UN General Assembly in September 1998, they agreed an exchange of statements according to which the Iranian government declared they would not take any action to threaten the life of the author of *The Satanic Verses* nor anyone associated with his work, and would not encourage or assist anybody to do so. Dr Kharrazi also dissociated the Iranian government from the bounty on Rushdie's life (and on the British side there were hopes that the better atmosphere between the two governments might soon lead to the bounty being withdrawn altogether). On this basis, the two sides agreed to exchange ambassadors for the first time since 1980, and a general thaw in relations became possible.

After the meeting in New York and the subsequent media excitement, there were some statements and other manifestations in Iran against the agreement reached there, but nothing worse than might have been anticipated. Equally, there was some doubt and dissent on the UK side, but nonetheless the exchange of ambassadors took place as agreed in May 1999. After some discussion, this took the form of raising to the status of ambassador the two chargés d'affaires who were in place in London and Tehran: Gholamreza Ansari and Nick Browne. And when

Cook and Kharrazi met again in September 1999, they agreed to visit each others' capitals. Dr Kharrazi duly visited London in January 2000. Robin Cook was scheduled to visit Tehran in May 2000 but was forced to postpone by a crisis in Zimbabwe, and attempts to make another date were frustrated by problems on Dr Kharrazi's side. Eventually, Jack Straw made the return visit after replacing Cook as foreign secretary.

Over this period, there were many visits in both directions by British and Iranian officials, including the senior civil servant in the Foreign Office, the permanent under-secretary Sir John Kerr, in November 1999 and Deputy Foreign Minister Sarmadi in March 2000. These visits paralleled EU–Iran meetings that began again after a decision by EU foreign ministers in March 1998, which stipulated that the dialogue should address matters of mutual interest as well as areas of concern. The first of these meetings took place in Tehran in July 1998. There were further meetings in Vienna in December 1998, in Tehran in May 1999, in Helsinki in December 1999 and in Tehran again in June 2000.

From the UK perspective, our impression was that there were mixed feelings within the Iranian government about the improvement of relations. In both his conduct of government and his public statements, President Khatami showed that he was serious about ending Iran's isolation and rebuilding contacts with Europe. Although his expression of this often appeared in an idealistic and philosophical idiom somewhat alien to the usual language of British politics and diplomacy, there was no doubting his sincerity. And as contacts improved, we quickly found common ground and scope for practical cooperation. In discussions about Iraq and Afghanistan, for example, we found a close identity between Iranian and British interests in greater stability, and out of the talks on Afghanistan there emerged valuable cooperation against drug trafficking. The British were also impressed by Iranian accounts of the pressure of the large number of refugees from Iraq and Afghanistan that had sought refuge in Iran (nearly two million people in all), and set about establishing programmes of assistance in that sector too. In addition, we began cooperation on the removal of landmines left on Iranian territory since the Iran–Iraq war. Discussions also focused on the expansion of our respective embassies, on the question of debts outstanding since the time of the 1979 revolution and on the return of the British Council to Iran.

Nonetheless, there were problems. Sometimes we were reminded of habits of mind on the Iranian side that had developed in the period of isolation. And despite the improvement in relations, we still had serious concerns in three main areas: human rights (especially the inadequacy of judicial proceedings, the use of torture, the imposition of inhumane punishments, the persecution of religious minorities and the use by state organs of extra-legal and non-constitutional powers), terrorism and the Iranian nuclear programme. These were delicate matters, but usually we could have a sensible discussion of them. For example, Robin Cook and Dr Kharrazi had a useful extended discussion of the Middle East peace process in London in January 1999, dwelling at some length on Iranian support for organizations that opposed the process with violence and on the question of a right of return for Palestinian refugees. In other discussions, on human rights, the Iranians claimed with some justice (and particularly in the treatment of women) that their record was significantly better than many other states in the region. But on other occasions, Iranian officials tried to deflect our questions on these and other matters by telling us baldly that we should not listen to the lies of the Mojahedin-e Khalq (MKO) organization.[2] Since we spent some time in London trying to convince British MPs and others that the MKO were an unreliable source of information on Iran, this was frustrating.

More seriously, it was plain that some elements in the Iranian system, notably in the Ministry of Information and Security (MOIS) but also in the Revolutionary Guard Corps and elsewhere, were opposed to the Khatami policy of *rapprochement* with the European Union in general and the United Kingdom in particular. This opposition emerged in some of the more hard-line parts of the Iranian press, generally aligned with the MOIS, where articles hostile to the United Kingdom and to closer ties with the United Kingdom were common. It also manifested itself in occasional reiterations from some quarters of attachment to the Rushdie fatwa, and, more trivially, seemed to play a part in the continual difficulties we had in obtaining visas for official visits. The Iranians imposed a ceiling on the number of our diplomatic staff, which meant, among other things, that our visa section in the embassy in Tehran was kept artificially small, much too small to cope with the demand for visas to visit the United Kingdom.

These matters generated problems and, inevitably, complaints from the Iranian side. Our perception was that whereas the reformist elements in the Iranian system favoured *rapprochement* for its own sake, the more hard-line and hostile elements had accepted the policy reluctantly. They had done so after the leadership had ruled (by a decision arbitrated through the Supreme National Security Council, which includes representatives from all elements of the Iranian government) that the policy should go ahead, primarily for the sake of encouraging inward investment. So through this period, we felt as though we had been invited to dinner by a warring couple. As we tried to enter the door, one of them was trying to open it and welcome us in, while the other was trying to jam it shut again.

This of course reflected the wider political position in Iran, as the reform process tried to make headway against opposition by those same hard-line elements. The British view from the beginning was that our remaining concerns about the relationship, particularly on terrorism and human rights, were most likely to be resolved if the drive for reform prospered. For example, if President Khatami succeeded in pushing through his declared programme for the rule of law and the establishment of civil society, most of our human rights concerns would disappear. We therefore watched the progress of the reform project with interest, and were encouraged by the strong support for it expressed by the Iranian people in successive elections. At all times, we had to bear in mind the need to avoid real or apparent interference in Iranian politics and to minimize the legitimate mistrust of the United Kingdom that many, if not most Iranians, felt as a legacy of the period of colonial interference, the 1953 coup and more recent episodes, such as the Iran–Iraq war and the West's handling of the Shia revolt in southern Iraq in 1991 after the liberation of Kuwait.

It was plain to us that the drive for inward investment was an important factor in Iran's foreign policy in 1997–2000. It was always at or near the top of the list of issues that the Iranians wanted to raise with us in meetings. They explained that they needed inward investment (especially in the non-oil sector) in order to create jobs, to reverse the trend of rising unemployment and to reduce the dependence of the Iranian economy on oil. We were sympathetic, and did what we could, but in the end British companies had to make their own judgements about the business case for investment in Iran. When companies came to us for advice, we were positive about prospects, but our ability to influence the general pattern of trade was slight. In 1998–2000, according to the figures we had at the time, the value of our bilateral trade actually declined.

There was a minor positive aspect to this: the figures were a good answer to our critics in Britain who told us that by improving ties with Iran, we were selling out human rights for the sake of trade. But medium-term export credit guarantee cover was restored in mid-2000, Shell secured an oil exploration project and other UK firms were showing serious interest. Like other aspects of the UK–Iran relationship, there were grounds for believing that trade was also set to improve. Of course, we welcomed this. The broad policy was that engagement with Iran was beneficial all round and that the longer it went on and prospered, the less likely retrograde movement would be. According to that view, economic and business contacts gave the Iranian regime something to lose, a vested interest in the continuation of good relations and, most importantly, a reason to change its policy in our remaining areas of concern.

One perennial question in Iranian foreign policy that lurked in the background throughout this period was the question of whether or not to resume diplomatic relations between Iran and the United States. On several occasions, President Khatami made statements that seemed to suggest an openness to renewed contact with the United States (most notably in an interview with Christiane Amanpour of CNN, broadcast in January 1998).[3] But it appeared that a block on a renewal of relations, like Iran's hostile attitude to Israel, had the character of immovable shibboleths for the hard-line elements in the Iranian regime: an inheritance from the revolution period. Some international commentators speculated that after the improvement of UK–Iran relations in autumn 1998, Britain would act as an honest broker between Iran and the United States. This was perhaps a natural thing to think, but the UK government never offered itself to either party in this role at this time; and to my knowledge neither Iran nor the United States ever made the request of us. It would have been difficult too for the US government to make a serious effort at *rapprochement*, although Clinton and his secretary of state Madeleine Albright made a number of conciliatory statements in 1999 and 2000. The United States took an interest in the progress of our contacts with Iran, but we never saw ourselves as a conduit for information.

Our perception of the intimate connection between Iranian foreign policy and internal politics was reinforced by a series of related incidents beginning in late 1998. The murders of writers and dissidents in Iran in November–December 1998, which became known afterwards as the serial murders, provoked a protest from the European Union and were interpreted by many as an attempt by hardliners in the MOIS to confront and discredit President Khatami. When he successfully faced down that attempt and secured the arrest of Saeed Emami and some of the other perpetrators, we judged that he had strengthened both his own position and the reform process. But the arrests were followed by the detention of 13 Jews and two Muslims in Shiraz on espionage charges, and our judgement was that disgruntled MOIS officials had arrested innocent people in order to present the organization as bravely resisting some kind of Zionist plot, while further embarrassing Iran's efforts at international *rapprochement.*

The question of the detainees and their uncertain future attracted criticism of Iran, and of our Iran policy, in the United Kingdom and the European Union generally. The concern that the detainees might be executed made many on the British side uncertain about pursuing closer contacts. It was not an encouraging episode, but we continued to believe that we were in a stronger position to protest over the detainees' plight and other continuing human rights abuses (notably the persecution of the Bahais) if we maintained the closer contacts we had enjoyed since autumn 1998. The steady strong support for President Khatami encouraged us to think that he would overcome the problems. Although some in the West were disillusioned when he sided with the hard-line leadership in summer 1999 and let them break up student protests, it seemed that many Iranians agreed with him that evolutionary change was better than violence. There was good reason to think that he was right: after the experience of one revolution, it was understandable that Khatami and many other Iranians were unwilling to risk their hopes for change on the outcome of street violence. Whatever went wrong, we were encouraged during this time by the vigour of the free press in Iran, which expanded on a scale that appeared unstoppable and became more and more bold in its criticisms of the regime and in its demands for change.

With the election of the strongly reformist Sixth Majlis in May 2000 (reform-orientated candidates secured 190 of 290 seats), many observers thought the reformists were in the driving seat at last. There was speculation that Iran might now move in the direction of a moderated form of religious supremacy, with the clerical element in the system guiding occasionally from the background[4] rather than taking a direct, foreground role as it had since 1979. But in retrospect, my personal view is that the attacks on former President Rafsanjani in that election campaign were a decisive error by the reformist press: they overreached themselves and drove an embittered Rafsanjani (who had previously tried rather ineffectually to arbitrate between the two camps) over to the hard-line side. From summer 2000, hard-line resistance to the reformist programme stiffened and became more competent, perhaps reflecting Rafsanjani's assistance. A sustained and cleverly targeted series of arrests and closures brought the flowering of the free press to an end.[5] Supreme Leader Ayatollah Ali Khamenei intervened personally to prevent the new Majlis from overturning the press law that facilitated this crackdown (it had been passed by the old Majlis in the last months of its term) and the Majlis generally found themselves blocked by hard-line elements in the Iranian system from making any significant progress with the reform programme. If ever Khatami missed the chance to confront the hard-line leadership (as was probably unavoidable if the reform project were to succeed), to follow through on his popular mandate for reform and to secure the future of his policy of international *rapprochement* along with it, this was surely the time. But the moment passed, the free press faded and the hard-line party regained confidence. The testing of the Shahab III medium-range missile in July 2000 also marked a new phase, of sharpened international concern over Iranian weapons programmes and nuclear ambitions.

Despite the reverses for the reformist faction, some of the changes brought in by President Khatami endured, not least Iran's more engaged, less isolated relationship with Europe and the wider world. Iran's relations with Britain were an important part of that; and the continuing strength of the contacts, especially when tested in the changed international atmosphere after September 2001, showed that the judgement of the two governments in summer 1998, that it was in their interests to improve relations, was correct. Since the election of President Ahmadinejad in June 2005, Iranian politics and international relations have entered a new phase, about which at present it is more difficult to be optimistic. But the experience of the years 1997–2000 shows at the very least the beginnings of the progress that can be achieved when even the most mistrustful partners decide to edge away from familiar, hostile positions that play to ingrained prejudices in their domestic politics and attempt instead to engage with each other.

NOTES

1 Since I have drawn mainly on personal memory I have not included extensive footnotes.

2 The MKO are designated as a terrorist organization in the United States and the European Union, and have sought to overthrow the regime in Iran since the early 1980s when they lost out in a power struggle after the revolution and went into exile. While in exile they discredited themselves within Iran by fighting alongside Saddam Hussein's forces in the Iran/Iraq war. For a comprehensive account of the MKO, see Ervand Abrahamian, *The Iranian Mojahedin* (Yale, 1992); also my article in *Prospect* magazine, March 2005, pp 15–17.

3 The interview is discussed in detail in Ali Ansari, *Iran, Islam and Democracy* (London: The Royal Institute of International Affairs, 2000), pp. 133–7.

4 As recommended by Ayatollah Hossein Ali Montazeri, the Titurel of Iranian Shiism (see, among other statements, the interview published in the *Mideast Mirror* on 20 January 2000, p. 15). Montazeri, despite being under house arrest, spoke out against any interference in the elections of May 2000. He appeared also to concur with the view of theologian Abdolkarim Soroush that too intimate an involvement in everyday politics risked discrediting religion among ordinary people.

5 For a discussion of the crackdown on the free press in summer 2000, see Ansari, *Iran, Islam and Democracy*, pp. 211–17.

8

Arab–Iranian Relations: New Realities?

Mahjoob Zweiri

Introduction

The Arab world and the Islamic Republic of Iran have many commonalities, such as history, religion, culture and geopolitics, and they also share a series of contemporary challenges. The war on terror and the invasion of Iraq in 2003 and its consequences have forced both sides to communicate directly with each other and to overlook the differences and tensions that have always beset their relations.

Both sides are well aware that many aspects of their relationship have yet to be resolved; and for their part, the Arab countries have contradictory attitudes towards Iran. Some states, such as Syria, have enjoyed good relations with it whereas others, including Saudi Arabia, Egypt and Jordan, see it as a threat to their national security. However, the member countries of the Gulf Cooperation Council (GCC) have shifted their stance and tried to normalize their relations with Iran, particularly after the reformist president Muhammad Khatami came to office in May 1997.

Iran's foreign policy since 1997 has proved that if it does not change how it deals with neighbouring Arab countries, its relationship with them will not progress. The Iranian attitude towards Jordan and Saudi Arabia confirms such a conclusion. On the other hand, Arab countries must acknowledge that Iran, and also Turkey, are important regional powers because without establishing normal relations with them, stability in the Middle East will be difficult to achieve. Nevertheless, they need a degree of reassurance from Iran about regional security. Accordingly, Iran has sent positive messages to several Arab countries, and this has helped to create trust between both sides.

Regional developments – the Iran–Iraq war of 1980–8, Iraq's invasion of Kuwait in 1990 and the ongoing conflict in Iraq – have shed light on the level of disagreement that exists between the Arab world and Iran. Crucial issues, such as Iran's wish to export its revolution, its interference in neighbouring countries' internal affairs and its support of Shia groups within Iraq and the GCC states have continued to dominate, and vex, Arab–Iranian relations.

Iraqi Politics and the Shia Dimension

Iraq has had a significant impact on Arab–Iranian relations since the Iranian revolution, and the eight-year war between Iraq and Iran formalized the character of the relationship between the two sides. Iraq, according to the Arab world, was protecting its 'eastern gate'. It was also limiting Iran's support for Shias in the Arab world. Iran, however, understood the war as an attempt to weaken the revolution; and as long as its Arab neighbours were helping Iraq, they would be treated as enemies of the new Islamic Republic. From 1979 to 1997, Arab countries such as Jordan, Egypt and the GCC countries had several concerns about Iran. First, it gave support to Shia minorities, which was considered as direct interference in their domestic affairs. Second, it continually criticized the strong ties between some Arab governments and the United States. Third, there were Iran's 'three islands' dispute with the United Arab Emirates about sovereignty over Abu Musa and the Tunbs, territorial problems between Iran and Qatar, Iraq and Kuwait and also contention about the name of the Gulf – 'Persian' or 'Arab'.

The invasion of Iraq has re-emphasized the significance of the Iraqi factor in the Arab–Iranian relationship. Iran had identified Iraq as the archetypal enemy since 1979, but it understood that the regime in Iraq was no longer accepted by the Gulf countries after its invasion of Kuwait. Iran was at one with the Gulf Arab states in opposing the invasion, and it used this to remind them of their mistake in supporting Saddam Hussein in his war against Iran in the 1980s. Besides showing its solidarity with Kuwait, Iran supported the bulk of international resolutions on Iraq. This attitude had an impact on some Arab countries: in fact, a majority of them renewed their diplomatic relations with Iran.

It became clear that every country in the Gulf region had considered the Iraqi regime as a threat to its own security and stability. This belief had facilitated the international policies against Iraq, and it was obvious that any military action against Iraq, even by Iran, would be favoured by regional governments.[1]

As a consequence of the invasion of Iraq in 2003, two main sources of tension have troubled Arab–Iranian relations. The first pertains to security. Iran is concerned about the presence of American forces in the region. The GCC is anxious about Iran's nuclear ambition and its impact on stability in the Gulf. The second source of worry is about political and social issues, including the emergence of a new political elite in Iraq and the re-emergence of the debate about identity and citizenship, which are becoming real challenges facing states in the Middle East. The GCC countries are also anxious about rising Shia aspirations in the region, which in turn have led to the emergence of Sunni militancy, often linked to al-Qaida which views the Shias as an enemy that have facilitated the invasion of Iraq by the United States.

Iran has its own concerns regarding the 160,000 American troops close to its border. Iran sees the conflict between Sunni and Shia, which reemerged after the American invasion of Iraq, affecting its image in the Sunni Muslim World, limiting any Iranian role in the wider Middle East. In addition to this, the American presence in the region is threatening Iran's own security, especially given the additional American presence in Afghanistan. However, Iran aims to benefit from this, especially when it comes to discussing the nuclear issue and possible US military action against its nuclear installations. It has been reported that Iran has sent a warning message by Recep Tayyip Erdoğan, the prime minister of Turkey, to the United States stating that thousands of American soldiers would be kidnapped if Iran were attacked.

Despite keeping diplomatic doors open to Baghdad during the 1980–8 war, Iran had limited its relations with Iraq because of un-resolved issues between the two countries, for instance the borders issue which remains unsolved. The possibility now arose of an end to the Iraqi Ba'ath regime. Iran also benefited from American intervention against another neighbour when its enemy to the east, the Taliban in Afghanistan, was toppled. Iran, as a Shia state, was satisfied that the American strategy of 'regime change' in Iraq brought Shias to power. It was also pleased that the Mujahideen-e-Khalq party, which seeks the overthrow of the Iranian government, had become weak after the collapse of Saddam's regime, which had supported it or at least allowed it to stay in Iraq.

Iran has showed its support for a post-Saddam Iraq, being second only to the United States in its support for the new Iraqi government.

Tehran has contributed $100 million to rebuilding Iraqi infrastructure. Tehran also has strong ties with the new Iraqi elite. This reality has encouraged Iran to be more involved in Iraqi politics.[2] It has cooperated with religious and secular Iraqis, to show that there is no Iranian aspiration to establish a religious state in Iraq and divide up the country. Iran has a strong relationship with Shia religious groups such the Supreme Council for the Islamic Revolution in Iraq and it has maintained ties with the secular Shia group the Iraqi National Congress, which is led by Ahmad Chalabi. It also has connections with the Patriotic Union of Kurdistan. It has worked with Iraq's neighbours to support the new government economically and politically.

The new Iraqi elite gives priority in Iraq's foreign policy to Iran, as shown by its many visits there. This is a result of the political isolation that those politicians suffered, especially at the hands of Arab governments. The former prime minister Ibrahim Jaafari, who spent years in exile in Iran and currently represents the Islamic Dawa party, which is supported and funded by Iran, visited Iran in July 2005,[3] and Nouri al-Maliki, the current prime minister, paid a visit to the Islamic Republic in September 2006. President Jalal Talabani visited Tehran too, in November 2006, and there are also regular trips there by Members of Parliament, ministers and military personnel. The only exception has been the interim prime minister Iyad Allawi, who was invited to visit Iran but did not go. It became clear that he was worried about Iran's role in Iraq.

The two countries have signed many agreements on different levels. Iran has promised to help rebuild Najaf airport and to connect the two countries' rail networks as a step towards increasing trade and religious tourism. A security agreement has been signed that will lead to the exchange of security information between the two sides. The new cooperation between Iraq and Iran might reflect the isolation to which the post-Saddam Iraqi politicians have been subjected, particularly by the GCC and other Arab states.

Iraq has become an arena of conflict between Arab and Iranian interests. The reason for this is the historical background of its politicians and their divisions based on religious and political aspirations. Most of the new political elite in Iraq has come from exile; its members have established strong relations with Iran, and none of this elite has had contacts with Arab countries except Kuwait, which has strong ties with the Supreme Council for the Islamic Revolution in Iraq.

It is important to note that there is a real conflict of interest between Arabs and Iranians, and this can clearly be seen within the new Iraqi elite. The current situation in Iraq presents a potential for rising tensions and divisions between the key 'political' Shia actors, notably Grand Ayatollah Sistani and Muqtada al-Sadr.[4] With Sistani coming from an Iranian background and al-Sadr being of Arab descent, there is a real danger that this division will be driven by the two actors' narrowly defined nationalistic sentiments. Conflict flared up when al-Sadr sought to incite the Shia community to fight against the Americans in Iraq.[5] Sistani stands at the other end of the spectrum, trying to pacify the same religious community as he appeals for calm and for support for the US-designed political policy for Iraq. Their differing backgrounds make the conflict deep-rooted, complex and difficult to solve. The clash between the two sides has resulted in the formation of different attitudes and perceptions among Shias towards the political process in the country.

The political identity of post-Saddam Iraq has been of much importance to the Arab states. Iran has welcomed the new political arrangements in Iraq. There was real support for the interim council that was formed after the invasion of Iraq, and Iran has also supported the election process in the country, and has respected the result of these elections. By contrast, GCC foreign ministers announced in September 2005 that the 'Iraqi people must preserve the Arab and Islamic identity of Iraq'.[6] The GCC states have not suggested that the new Iraq ought to become part of the GCC, even though plans for Yemen's membership have been discussed. This has widened the gap between Iraq and the GCC, and may push the former's political elite towards Iran. Clearly, the GCC states are concerned about an insecure and unstable Iraq joining them at this stage.

Developments in Iraq since 2003 have led to two fundamental changes. First, the Salafi Jihadi school has emerged as a threat to the security of the Gulf. This was as a result of the cooperation of some of the GCC governments with the international coalition in the invasion of Iraq. Second, there has been a real change in the image of Shias in the Middle East. In the 1980s the Shia were presented by the United States as a threat to the security of the Middle East and GCC region. Today, the Shia in the new Iraq are the ally of the United States. This change does not apply to the governments of the Middle East and the GCC, which still consider the Shia-led government in Iraq to be a new security challenge, at least to some extent.

Among the Arab states, the prospect of a Shia-led government influenced by Iran represents a real threat. As a consequence, mistrust has arisen between the Arab countries and Iraqi politicians. For example, when Ghazi al-Yawar, the Sunni Arab shaykh, was selected as Iraq's interim president, he was welcomed in regional capitals as a 'Sunni leader'. At the same time, Iran was welcoming Shia leaders to Tehran. It has showed support for post-2003 governments of all kinds, but in fact it was not happy about working with Iyad Allawi and later with Nouri al-Maliki because both individuals had Arab nationalist aspirations.

The possible extent and consequences of Iran's influence has become the core issue of debate between the United States and some of the Iraqi leaders who are displeased about that influence, seeing it as interference. Its influence has also been the focus of talks between Arab leaders and the new Iraqi elite. After al-Yawar visited Jordan in December 2004 and warned King Abdullah about Iranian influence in Iraq, a US administration official involved with policy towards Iraq commented on the fact that the Sunni role had been marginalized in post-Saddam Iraq and that 'it touches emotional, religious and historic chords and signifies changes they [Arab leaders] don't like . . . It's a big emotional hurdle for the Sunnis in the region to accept.'[7] At the most senior level, King Abdullah of Jordan has warned of a 'Shia crescent' 'stretching from Iran all the way through Iraq to Syria and Lebanon',[8] and President Husni Mubarak has admitted that Iran 'exerted strong influence over Iraq's majority Shia population and Shias living in other Arab countries'.[9]

There is no doubt that Iran is central to this. Very soon after the fall of Baghdad, President Khatami went to Beirut.[10] He was received there by jubilant crowds and gave a talk at a stadium attended by 50,000 people. It is safe to say that not since Gamal Abdal Nasser in the 1950s has a foreign leader generated so much enthusiasm in Lebanon. Iran is important in this context because it is the largest Shia country and is the 'superpower' of Shia politics in the Middle East.[11] It is impossible for the United States to consider what might be the implications of Shia empowerment across the region without considering how Iran will fit in and how its own role will be affected. Shia empowerment is also happening at a time when Iran's claims to be a regional power have been gaining a greater voice in the midst of the nuclear tussle with the United

States. Iran sees itself, as is evident concerning the nuclear issue, in a completely different light, and the empowerment of the Shias fits in with that. But as relations between the United States and Iran have deteriorated, Iran has gradually found itself at the centre of a Sunni call to resist Shia empowerment. For example, there is already resistance to political reform in Lebanon, Saudi Arabia and Bahrain, and the worry is not that it will empower the Shias but that it will empower Iran. For this reason, Iran, whatever it wishes, is going to be central to debates about the future of Shia movements in the Middle East.

Lebanon will be one of the key countries in this matter. The Shias there constitute, according to the lowest estimates, about 45 per cent of the population. Lebanon has been undergoing a degree of political reform in the aftermath of the assassination of the former prime minister Rafik Hariri in 2005 and the withdrawal of Syrian troops. The issue of Shia power is on the table, with Hezbollah becoming more powerful since Syria's withdrawal. The Gulf states, especially Kuwait, Bahrain and Saudi Arabia, have Shia populations which are becoming more assertive in the post-Saddam era. The Gulf Shias have historically been dismissed and neglected, and therefore it will be interesting to see how their greater political assertiveness is dealt with in the context of changing regional politics.

The Arab World between Reformists and Neoconservatives in Iran

Mahmoud Ahmadinejad was elected as the sixth president of Iran on 24 June 2005. His conservative reputation has created a new wave of concern in the Arab world and has made Iran's foreign policy an important issue for the international community. There has been an increasing desire to know its direction, especially with regard to the Arab states.

During the eight-year period of Ahmadinejad's predecessor Muhammad Khatami, Iran's foreign policy had two principal emphases: creating strong links between domestic issues and foreign policy and improving international interactions through the policy of détente and mutual respect. By changing the negative view of Iran, Khatami improved both the image of the ayatollahs and Iran's standing in the international community and with the Arab world. By 2001, his initiative, the Dialogue among Civilizations, accorded increased respect to him personally and also to Iran. This new attitude towards Khatami, as a leader of reform, replaced the previously existing belief that Iran's foreign policy was 'closely connected to, and indeed an extension of, policies and priorities of the theocratic regime and its dominant elite'.[12]

The change within the domestic politics of Iran was not understood by the Arab elite, and so it seems that Iran remains a threat to the Arab states whether it is ruled by traditional conservatives, reformists or neoconservatives. According to a majority of Arab politicians, Iran is a trouble-making country whose decision-makers always remain the same, whoever is in power. Simply because they belong to the same revolutionary institution, this belief has closed the doors to any attempt to understand Iranian politics.

When President Khatami came to office, his attitudes were well received by the Arab world, but at the same time it hid its real concern about his statements on the role of nations and religious democracy. By calling for more democracy and people's participation in the decision-making process, he was indirectly criticizing those Arab regimes which have continued to ignore the role of their own people. In other words, he was criticizing the authoritarian way of governing in the Middle East. His policy of opening up to the West was viewed as a way to compete with the Arab states, and his discourse was seen as stemming from nationalist desires. Moreover, the image presented of the Iranian leadership was perceived as an attempt to undermine the image of Arab leaders. For example, Imam Khomeini's populist approach when speaking about Islam, Palestine and the United States had allowed him to be embraced by the Arab masses as a much-needed hero. He had succeeded in winning a majority of Arab hearts and minds. Khatami too gained immense respect among Arab thinkers and politicians.

President Ahmadinejad has also become a regional hero, not only in the Arab 'street' but also in the wider Islamic world. His background, appearance and criticism of the United States and Israel appeals to Muslim masses around the globe.[13] There is no doubt that the religious image of these politicians influences any progress in relations between the two sides.

Iran's Nuclear Programme and Arab Countries

President Ahmadinejad, like the rest of the political system in Iran, believes that the country's nuclear programme is a question of life and death. 'Iran has the full right to have a peaceful nuclear technology for energy, medical and agricultural purposes and scientific progress'; this is the 'the right of the Iranian nation'.[14] Furthermore, he has promised that while his government will have 'fresh nuclear policies',[15] it will still respect the position taken by the Khatami government. And any changes that are made will come about because decisions on this issue are made by the four leaders of Iran (the supreme leader, the president, the leader of the judiciary and the speaker of the Majlis). The former foreign minister Kamal Kharrazi has suggested that Ahmadinejad will also adopt 'the same course . . . particularly with regards to international détente and cooperation'.[16] Although Ahmadinejad, as president, might change the negotiating team for the nuclear programme, this should not affect the negotiation process.

Iran's decision to resume nuclear development at the Isfahan site just days before Ahmadinejad came to office was a sign that the ongoing crisis concerning the Iranian nuclear programme was to be accelarated. It is over the nuclear issue that the former government tried to create trouble for the incumbent. Arguably, this step was a tactic to change the image of the president and his government in the European Union and the United States. But on the first day of his presidency, Ahmadinejad agreed to delay resuming the nuclear programme by 48 hours.

The decision to resume nuclear activities put pressure on the European Union and simultaneously provided evidence that Iran was serious about finding a solution to this crisis. Iran knew that the European Union would not be happy but went ahead regardless of any consequence that might be caused by the announcement that the International Atomic Energy Agency had been informed of its decision. The consequence of this decision was that the whole issue was transferred to the United Nations Security Council. The threat of Security Council sanctions, according to Iranian officials, shows that the European Union does not have the initiative to participate or to act as a partner in these discussions. This contradicts the widely held belief that the European Union and the United States are able to find solutions without recourse to sanctions or military action. In this context, it is necessary to remind ourselves of the political machinations behind the war in Iraq, especially as it has been confirmed that Iraq did not possess any weapons of mass destruction.

Iran under President Ahmadinejad has in fact changed the whole perception of its nuclear programme. His political attitude, especially towards Israel and the Holocaust, has helped the United States to mobilize not only European countries but also China, Russia and the Arab world against Iran.

The European Union's concerns are based on Iran's radical policies regarding publications and the government's interference in people's lives. These concerns increased as soon as Ahmadinejad became president. However, he indicated at his first press conference that his 'government will pursue moderation at the national level' and emphasized that 'there is no room for radicalism in [my] government and the pursuit of radicalism will be confronted'.[17]

Even though the president has very limited authority over Iran's foreign policy, it is nonetheless affected by his performance and character. His press releases and interviews show the direction in which he wants to take the country. Contradictions are to be expected in his messages to the Iranian people and to the international community. Ahmadinejad must also face a radical contingent which is not happy with the resumption of enriching uranium in Isfahan. This contingent blames Khatami's negotiations with the European Union concerning the Iranian nuclear programme because of Khatami's initiative to suspend the uranium enrichment in 2004. Iran needs to show that future discussions with the European Union will not be affected by this faction.

Iran's support of America in the Afghanistan and Iraq wars is a reminder that it can respond to the United States as an ally. However, it remains essential to hold direct talks with the Americans.[18] The first direct talks between Washington and Tehran for a long time were held in Baghdad on 28 April 2007. This round of talks focused on the issue of Iraq and how Iran could help in stabilizing its neighbour. There was no mention of the bilateral issues.[19]

At some stage, progress was made in the US–North Korean negotiations as a way to find a solution to the nuclear issues between them. Iran and the United States need to think along the same lines, particularly as the latter, in cooperation with the European Union, submitted an offer to Iran on 5 August 2005 promising a 'full political and economic relationship with the West, if Iran ends nuclear activities suspected to be part of a weapons program'.[20] This offer came just after a report published by the *Washington Post* had stated that Iran is 'about 10 years away from manufacturing the key ingredients for a nuclear weapon'.[21] The timing of this report is highly significant, as it came just several days before the hardliner Ahmadinejad acceded to office in 2005. Recent reports, however, have suggested that Iran is only four years away from acquiring an atomic bomb.[22]

Arab countries, as well as the European Union and the United States, expressed concern about Iran as a threat to security in the Middle East soon after Ahmadinejad came to power. These states, including Jordan, Egypt and the GCC countries, have not hidden their worry about an Iranian nuclear programme and the policy Iran is following. The GCC countries are anxious about three main issues: the Russian technology used by Iran, the programme's environmental impact and also the possibility of its acceleration and an American attack on Iran.

These concerns have been articulated by Arab officials and GCC countries. The foreign minister of Saudi Arabia has announced that the Iranian nuclear programme is not a threat to their countries, but at the same time he has asked Iran to pay more attention to the demands of the international community. Egypt takes the same position. Interestingly, the secretary of the Arab league has criticized Arab countries for not doing enough to have their own nuclear programmes so that they can join the nuclear club and follow the examples of Pakistan and India. He stated at the eighteenth annual Arab summit, held in Khartoum on 28 March 2006, that 'it is important for me to use this forum to call on the Arab World to quickly and powerfully enter the world of using nuclear power'.[23] Abdul Rahman al-Attiya, Secretary-General of the Gulf Cooperation Council, announced on 22 February 2007 that he and other GCC officials may travel to Vienna to seek help for the six GCC countries to start using nuclear power for peaceful purposes.[24]

The GCC countries believe that the technology used in the Bushehr nuclear site is not safe. They also believe that Iran's nuclear capability is real, unlike in the case of Iraq, and that an American air strike will lead to more escalation. Possible US military action would have real impact on the environment in their countries.

The change of Arab attitude towards nuclear technology seems significant. There is no doubt that in view of Iran's determination to have this technology despite the strong opposition of international powers and 'Israel having [all] but declared it has nuclear weapons capability',[25] the Arab states ought to make a decision to follow the nuclear path. It seems also that the price of oil has forced these countries to think seriously about using nuclear technology to tackle the future energy challenge.

However, according to Mahmud Nasreddin, Director-General of the Arab Atomic Energy Agency, 'the countries that have oil are not in a hurry to start a programme to build nuclear power plants tomorrow, but they are interested in feasibility studies'.[26]

According to the International Atomic Energy Agency, six Arab states are already involved in developing nuclear energy. These countries are Egypt, Morocco, Saudi Arabia, Algeria, Tunisia and the United Arab Emirates. Experts believe that the reason for their involvement is 'to provide the Arabs with [a] security hedge'.[27] Jordan has now joined these states, to become the seventh Arab country which plans 'to construct a nuclear reactor for peaceful purposes'.[28] It is to start production in 2015.[29]

Despite the fact that all the aforementioned Arab states are allies of the United States, their plans to use nuclear technology have not been welcomed by the Bush administration. The Arab states seem to feel that America and the international community do not 'do enough' about Iran and Israel. They also face pressure from their own people, who feel that they should have a nuclear capability, and they see that Iran, Israel, Pakistan and India are not economically better off than some of the Arab states. The Arabs thus wonder why Arab countries should remain excluded from the nuclear club.

As Arab states move towards nuclear technology, the balance of power will change. Their nuclear power status will add further complexity to the situation in the Middle East, which is already very complicated. The role of external actors is an element in the balance of power too. The relations between the Arab states and the United States do not help the former to move quickly towards nuclear technology. The consideration that Israel should keep its superiority is the most likely reason behind that.

The Iranian nuclear programme has been used to mobilize Arab states against the 'Iranian threat', but there is no mention of the Israeli threat to Arab national security. This perspective is creating the basis for a coalition between the 'moderate' states (Egypt, Jordan, Saudi Arabia and even the other GCC countries) with Israel to face the emerging Iranian threat. Such a coalition would meet America's desire to see regional cooperation against so-called Iranian expansion.

There is no doubt that the consequences of the war in Iraq have helped the United States to convince all its allies in the Middle East that Iran is the threat, not Israel. Iran's continuing intervention in Iraq justifies this American perception. Phobias about Iran and Shias, which have recently come to dominate the political climate in Arab countries, make it difficult to build bridges between Arab capitals and Tehran. The three mentioned factors, Iran's domestic politics, its nuclear programme and the Shia dimension have pushed Arab countries away from Iran and will continue to do so.

NOTES

1   The former commander of the Iraqi Republican Guard, Saif al-Din al-Rawi, has admitted that President Rafsanjani had encouraged Iraq to stay in Kuwait and promised Qusi Saddam Hussein Iranian help. According to al-Rawi, Rafsanjani promised to send Revolutionary Guards to fight side by side with the Iraqi army. He also asked them to send Iraqi aircraft, to hide them in Iran. Interview broadcast by Al Jazeera in Arabic on 7 April 2007.
2   Mahjoob Zweiri, 'Iran's Presence in Iraq: New Realties?', http://www.jcss.org/ UploadEvents/69.pdf, 14 May 2007.
3   Andy Mosher and Robin Wright, 'Iran, Iraq Herald "New Chapter" in Shiite-Led Alliance', www.washingtonpost.com, 17 July 2005.
4   See Juan Cole, 'The United States and Shi'ite Religious Factions in Post-Ba'thist Iraq', *The Middle East Journal*, vol. 57, no. 4 (Autumn 2003), pp. 550–2.
5   See 'The US–Shia Relationship in a New Iraq: Better than the British', *Strategic Insights*, Center for Contemporary Conflict, May 2004.
6   Bahrain News Agency, http://english.bna.bh/, 7 September 2005.
7   *The New York Times*, 15 December 2004.
8   Suha Ma'ayeh, 'Make up, make up', http://weekly.ahram.org.eg/2005/ 736/re2.htm, 6 April 2005 and Suha Ma'ayeh, 'Fear of a Shia full moon', http://www.guardian. co.uk/elsewhere/journalist/story/0,,1999399,00.html, 26 January 2007.
9   'Mubarak: US must not leave Iraq yet', http://english.aljazeera.net/English/ archive/archive?ArchiveId=21857, 10 April 2006.
10 V. Nasr, 'Iran and the Shia Revival in the Middle East', Rush Transcript, Federal News Service, March 2006.
11 Idem.
12 Zeba Moshaver, 'Revolution, Theocratic Leadership and Iran's Foreign Policy: Implications for Iran–EU Relations', *The Review of International Affairs*, vol. 3, no. 2 (Winter 2003), p. 283.
13 Roula Khalaf, 'Ahmadinejad cultivates image as regional hero', http://news. ft.com/cms/s/4f166918-e0f7-11da-90ad-0000779e2340,s01=1.htm, 11 May 2006.
14 'Iran to maintain nuclear policy', www.irna.ir, 8 June 2005.
15 'Iran will have new nuke, foreign policy ideas: Ahmadinejad', www.hindustantimes. com.
16 Idem.
17 *Iran Daily*, 27 July 2005.
18 There have been many attempts since former president Mohammad Khatami was elected in May 1997. His political approach to open up with the West, and his

new vision of Iran had helped to encourage holding direct talks and to normalize relations between Iran and the United States. However, all that took place before the war on Afghanistan and the invasion of Iraq. One of the still active projects is the Search for Common Ground programme, which aims to explore the possibility for better relations. For more information, see http://www.sfcg.org/programs/iran/programs_iran.html.

19   Mahjoob Zweiri, 'American-Iranian Talks on Iraq. End of Conflict or another Start?', http://www.jcss.org/UploadEvents/74.pdf, 31 May 2007.
20   *New York Times*, 5 August 2005.
21   *Washington Post*, 2 August 2005.
22   David Blair, 'Iran four years from atomic bomb', www.telegraph.co.uk, 24 April 2007.
23   *Al-Ittihad*, 29 March 2006 and http://www.arabtimesonline.com/arabtimes/diwaniya/view.asp?msgID=978, 20 March 2007.
24   'Persian Gulf states to move ahead with nuclear energy plans', www.iht.com, 11 February 2007.
25   'Arab nuclear ambitions stir arms race jitters', www.Khaleejtimes.com, 11 February 2007.
26   Idem.
27   Richard Beeston, 'Six Arab states join rush to go nuclear', www.timesonline.co.uk, 2 November 2006.
28   'Jordan plans nuclear energy by 2015', www.globes.co.il, 1 April 2007.
29   For more information about the nuclear capabilities of Arab states, see Sammy Salama and Heidi Weber, 'The Emerging Arab Response to Iran's Unabated Nuclear Program', www.nti.org, 22 December 2006.

9

Iran and its Immediate Neighbourhood

Anoushiravan Ehteshami

Introduction

For some years now, Iraq and its relations with its Persian Gulf neighbours have been amongst Iran's main foreign policy concerns. Over long periods since the early 1970s Iraq has not only challenged Iran's regional ambitions and tried to isolate it in the Arab world but has posed a direct security threat to its territorial integrity. Regime change in Iran in 1979 did not remove the tension between the parties, and eight years of war merely underscored the depth of animosity between them. Regime change in Iraq in 2003 certainly did change the relationship, however, prior to this regime change, the long conflict and absence of a formal peace treaty with Iraq had helped to intensify Iran's policy dilemmas towards Baghdad.

The Kuwait crisis of the early 1990s further complicated Tehran's worries about Iraq as a politically challenging and, potentially, militarily superior neighbour. Like the United States, Iran has been unable since 1991 to find suitable solutions to the range of shared security challenges presented by Iraq: weapons of mass destruction, territorial encroachment and fear of the possible consequences should Iraq disintegrate, all of which have been preoccupations for both Tehran and Washington. Other challenges, such as Baghdad's support for opponents of the Islamic regime and the effects of domestic Iraqi ethnic divisions on Iran, were worries for Iran alone. The longevity and continuity of Iran's problems with Iraq stand in stark juxtaposition to Tehran's singular failure until 2003/4 to deliver a consistent set of policy options towards Iraq. As a consequence, Iran ended up developing a short-termist attitude towards Iraq, even though the Iraqi state itself, its behaviour, and Iran's relations with its government and people continued to leave deep marks on Iran and its security-related calculations.

Despite their obvious differences, however, the two countries have interacted quite intensively throughout the whole period.[1] The first point to make is that Iran and Iraq have not been destined to be rivals. As events since the end of the 1980s have shown, the notion that ancient geopolitical animosities underline relations between the modern states of Iran and Iraq is little more than a myth. If the differences between these two neighbouring former empires are truly embedded in age-old quarrels, how then might the strategic partnership between secular Syria and Islamist Iran, or even that between imperial Iran (that is, before the revolution) and Israel, be explained? Thus, the tension in Iranian–Iraqi relations in modern times has virtually nothing to do with the Ottoman–Persian competition over Mesopotamia or theological and ideological differences between Sunnis and Shias, even though both sides have used historical events to justify their actions. Since the end of their war in 1988, Iran and Iraq have demonstrated remarkable capacities to cooperate with each other while also competing at the strategic level. This pattern of behaviour cannot be said to be characteristic of ancient animosities. Just as the friendship between Damascus and Tehran since 1980 has arisen out of shared objectives and fears, it was because of mutual suspicion and fear that the distance between Tehran and Baghdad was not bridged. In order to disentangle Iranian–Iraqi relations it must be accepted that tensions between Iraq and Iran have arisen as a consequence of the compounding of lingering problems by contemporary factors. Among these contemporary factors, one has had an overwhelming influence on Iranian–Iraqi relations – that is to say the Iranian revolution. Such an earthquake as a revolution was bound to seriously disrupt relations between Shia-dominated Iran and the only Shia-majority neighbouring country ruled by an Arab, nationalist-secular, Sunni-dominated, one-party dictatorship. Even though the revolution removed one of the West's strongest regional allies and Baghdad's strongest Persian Gulf rival from the scene, it should not have been surprising that Iraq's considered response was not one of jubilation. The hostility that the revolution generated in Iraqi circles should have been seen as inevitable, given the challenge that the new regime in Tehran posed, and that Iraq was forced to trade the known quantity of the Shah for the unknown factor of Ayatollah Khomeini.

Furthermore, as history has shown, revolutions do have a habit of creating geopolitical earthquakes in their wake, and this one did just that. It disrupted the security envelope in the region to such a degree as to cause a backlash from the neighbouring countries. Iraq's response was an extreme and aggressive one: direct military assault. As Iraq had tended to behave as a status quo power in the late 1970s Baghdad saw the Iranian revolution as a direct challenge to its regional role. By the same token, the emergence of the Gulf Cooperation Council in 1981 was the defensive response of a group of vulnerable Arab monarchies. In one way or another, however, virtually all of Iran's immediate neighbours responded to the Iranian revolution with a large dose of fear.

The second contemporary factor to note is the importance of Iraqi–Iranian relations for Persian Gulf security as a whole. Tehran and Baghdad have in the past tended to formulate their Gulf policies with one eye on each other and the other on the United States. Moreover, there has been enough irony in the recent history of Iranian and American approaches towards Iraq, and of their mutual responses to these policies, as to make this relationship central to security parameters of this vital sub-region.[2] In the 1980s, for example, Iran's military aim and strategic goal was to topple President Saddam Hussein and his regime and overthrow the Ba'ath Party-dominated state machinery of Iraq. This costly effort failed. For all the sacrifices made during the war, Khomeini had to finally drink from the 'poisoned chalice' and accept a ceasefire with Saddam Hussein and his regime. Iran's efforts came to naught largely for two reasons: Iran's blunders on the battlefield and in the diplomatic arena, and the strategic and political support that the United States and its allies were prepared to lend Iraq in its campaign against the Islamic Republic. Saddam Hussein outmanoeuvred and survived both his twentieth-century foes, Khomeini and President George H. W. Bush, by skilfully turning Iraq's geopolitical weaknesses into virtues, and also by being able to play the tensions between Tehran and Washington to his advantage.

In the 1990s, by contrast, it was Washington that set itself the military aim of isolating Iraq, with the strategic option of overthrowing the Ba'athist regime. While Iran would have welcomed these US efforts, Tehran was unable to lend much direct support. The reason was simple and understandable: Iran was in the containment zone with Iraq and had no incentive to help the United States gain the upper hand. Why should it strengthen the isolation of Iraq when that isolation squeezed Iran as well?

The 'dual containment' structure by which the United States put Iran in the same policy box as Iraq was a rough and ready solution to American security dilemmas in the Gulf. However, because it was obvious to all that Tehran and Washington feared the same enemy, it did not make sense to the Iranians to be placed alongside their mutual enemy, which ultimately meant that Iran did what it could to minimize the impact of dual containment on its intended targets. But dual containment also did not trigger a closer liaison between Tehran and Baghdad – largely because of the lingering differences between Iran and Iraq. In other circumstances, dual containment could well have produced a closer (anti-US) relationship between Tehran and Baghdad, which would have dramatically altered the regional balance of power – in ways that we have seen since in fact since 2003.

As dual containment faded away with the departure of the Clinton administration, Tehran hoped that a better working relationship could be established with the new Republican White House. Despite some evidence of flexibility on both sides, however, Iran's anxiety, to put it mildly, was heightened after January 2002, when it again found itself portrayed as Iraq's bedfellow, this time in a new 'axis of evil'. The difference, however, was a very significant one. While the containment policy had sought to isolate Tehran and curtail its regional influence, Iran believed that the new 'axis' language more directly targeted specific ruling regimes as 'evil' powers that should be removed. President George W. Bush's new 'doctrine' therefore was seen in Tehran as an existential threat to the Islamic Republic. As a result, Iran begun slowly to re-evaluate its calculations about the United States and Washington's regional ambitions – specifically as to how it could delay an inevitable confrontation.

The 2007 US National Intelligence Estimate, concluding that Iran had frozen its nuclear weapons programme back in 2003, has provided yet another new twist in this tripartite relationship. On the one hand, it is clear that the United States' initial successes in the Iraq war had encouraged Iran to suspend their nuclear weapons-related activities. The arrival of the United States on Iran's border was rightly seen as a formidable challenge by Tehran. But as much of the international narrative since 2003 has been on the American concerns about Iran's nuclear programme and ambitions, as a result of the 2007 NIE which assessed Iran's weapons programme as suspended, not only was the Bush administration forced to provide a defence of its confrontational stance towards Tehran subsequent to the publication of the main findings of this report, but equally the GCC countries – who until late 2007 were expressing their belief that Iran was pursuing a weapons programme – have had to backtrack and try and make amends with a strong populist Iranian leadership around President Ahmadinejad. If the Americans apparently assess that Iran is not pursuing a weapons programme, the argument went, then who are we to challenge them! The result: a strong case, made also by the Iraqi government, for the inclusion of Iran in all Gulf-related matters conducted by the GCC states. The Iranian president's presence at the GCC heads of state summit in Doha in December 2007 – the first time that an Iranian leader had been present in this closed shop – coincided with the NIE report and provided the opportunity for the parties to try and draw a line under a very tense period in their relations. Nonetheless, it is clear from the GCC side that their alliance with the United States remains critical and not subject to an Iranian veto. Therefore, the tensions between Tehran and Washington can still potentially adversely affect Iran–GCC relations. But it is again Iraq which can play a significant balancing role in this tussle.

The Legacy of the Iran–Iraq War

These recent developments ought to be viewed within a wider context, however. The backdrop to Iranian–Iraqi relations today is still largely the legacy left by the 1980–88 war. Many Iranians now in positions of power and influence served at the front and still speak bitterly of the war years. They openly cursed Saddam Hussein for the damage inflicted on their country and for the misery he brought to them personally, to their families, and to their associates. They celebrated in a very public manner when the Iraqi leader was hanged at the hands of Iraq's new, pro-Iranian, leaders for many Iranians regard the war as the root cause of the economic and social problems they now face; by extension, they hold the former Iraqi regime responsible for these current difficulties.

The war's broader impact can be divided into two sets of domestic developments, socioeconomic and security related. With regard to the former, the war created a vast national welfare network that now provides an impressive range of benefits for the families of war victims. From easier access to education, to employment and financial benefits, wartime service became a social ladder that veterans or their families could climb. This in turn produced vested interests that have proved quite resistant to change. These forces stand to gain from the legacy of the war, as has been demonstrated by the election of the war veteran Dr Ahmadinejad to the presidency in 2005.

A further social legacy of the war has been the culture of remembrance and commemoration – from the fountain of blood (oozing out red liquid) at the entrance of Tehran's main war cemetery, to streets named after war heroes, to the regularity with which key dates and events of the war are marked. People are continually reminded of the war, though the physical scars of eight years of conflict have all but disappeared. As a result, no government spokesperson could easily have supported revision of attitudes toward Iraq until it was clear that Iraq itself had changed.

The simple opening of borders to civilian traffic had far-reaching consequences. For one thing, it added an ethical and moral dimension to Iran's attitude toward Iraq; Tehran increasingly had to account for the growing sympathy of ordinary Iranian travellers for the plight of Iraqi and Shia citizens whom they saw suffering from UN sanctions and at the hands of their own government. The Iranian media routinely report on the suffering of the Iraqi people and often point to opportunities for state-to-state donations to the Iraqi people. Also, a rapid and large influx of Iranians into southern Iraq has introduced an Iranian economic influence and presence, as well as cash, into this strategic part of Iraq. Not only is the Iranian rial now traded there, but many Iranian goods are bought and sold throughout the southern half of Iraq. This unexpected economic leverage over Iraq has been a surprise to Tehran, which has made no particular use of it yet.

Secondly, with regard to security, regional tensions from Afghanistan to Palestine provide the backdrop of Iran's strategic thinking on the Persian Gulf subregion, and on Iraq in particular. Iran's strategic thinking and policy calculations are best understood through a levels-of-analysis approach, a composite in which domestic, regional and international factors all play roles.

On the domestic front, while time seems to be healing some of the wounds of the war, Iran remains cautious. There is a real fear in Tehran that the new Iraqi establishment, for reasons related to both domestic factors and its deep-rooted regional ambitions, remains close to an anti-Iran US establishment. Nevertheless, there are those who argue that it is in Iran's long-term interest to rapidly improve Iraqi relations, particularly while Baghdad remains vulnerable and weak. A closer relationship with Iraq, they argue, would give Iran a bigger say in Iraq's future, produce leverage over the current regime in Baghdad, and enable it to weaken the US presence in the area more generally. And also, of course, give Iran the upper hand in the Persian Gulf. But the proponents of the 'Iraq first' strategy are still having to justify this drive in the context of Iran's increasingly complex relationship with its other Arab neighbours and also Turkey.

The Decisive Triangle: Iran, Iraq and the United States
With the Taliban gone and Iran's northern borders relatively quiet, instability in Iraq has emerged as the most immediate security concern for Tehran. Another cause of concern for Iran is the cross-border military operations of the Iraq-based Mojahedin-e Khalq Organization (MKO), an Iranian dissident organization that was formed in the 1960s but today opposes the clerical Tehran regime with propaganda and terrorism.[3] Over the last few years the Iranian armed forces have been bold enough to attack MKO sites deep inside Iraq with aircraft and missiles, a pattern that, in the absence of a formal peace treaty between Tehran and Baghdad, is likely to continue. Tehran's Iraqi Shia allies (notably the Supreme Council for the Islamic Revolution in Iraq, or SCIRI, and its Badr Brigade) have regularly mounted anti-MKO operations.[4]

From the Iraqi perspective, there is also concern that the Iranian Revolutionary Guards (the Sepah) are awaiting a chance to test the Iraqi government's grip on the south. Should violence erupt, Baghdad fears that the Sepah may engage in some manner of low-key intervention on behalf of the pro-Iran Shia forces. It would therefore make sense to Baghdad to keep the MKO as its own reserve shock troops.

Another factor with a direct bearing on Iran's relations with Iraq is Tehran's deepening links with the GCC countries. Tehran has been able to demonstrate real progress in its relations with its Gulf Arab neighbours; in particular, it has tried to separate its dispute over three Persian Gulf islands with the United Arab Emirates from its broader confidence building with Saudi Arabia, Kuwait, Oman and Qatar.[5] Oman and Saudi Arabia have been its favourite partners, and Tehran is building on the warm political relations with them to develop military cooperation; until 2005 at least, joint exercises, visits and exchanges had become fixed items on the armed forces' agendas.[6] Iran's defence minister under President Khatami, Rear Admiral Ali Shamkhani, had championed improving relations with the GCC states as a way of blunting political attacks on Iran by the United States and of removing its pretexts for intervention, or indeed continuing military presence in the Persian Gulf. His calls for new Persian Gulf security arrangements were adopted by the political leadership and were built upon by the Khatami administration. Shamkhani said in 1997 that the Persian Gulf littoral states 'should seriously opt for formulation of a stable and coordinated strategy to reach sustainable security without foreign involvement'.[7] The Army and Iranian political leaders even told the Omani Air Force commander, Brigadier General Mohammed bin Mahfouz, during a visit in the summer of 1998 that Iran would be prepared to exchange its missile technology know-how with its Gulf Arab neighbours in exchange for a binding non-aggression and military cooperation accord. Oman, within the GCC forum, has expressed its interest in Iran's overtures in the military field. The Army's enthusiasm for a collective security pact in the Persian Gulf and the lengths it is prepared to go to make this Iran's declared policy was again highlighted in May 1999, during the official visit of Prince Sultan, Saudi Arabia's defence minister, to Tehran. Greeting him at Tehran's Mehrabad Airport, Admiral Shamkhani broke protocol and pressed the collective security issue in a one-on-one exchange with the prince before his political masters had a chance to see him. Some of this theme has continued with Khatami's successor. President Ahmadinejad's unprecedented participation at the GCC heads of state summit in Doha in December 2007, to talk about confidence building and deeper security cooperation, is a case in point. His presence (and acceptance) stems from the line adopted in the 1990s. It may have been followed somewhat erratically since 2005 but evidence suggests that it remains a cornerstone of the regime's regional policy.

In addition, Tehran is seriously concerned that the United States' current attitude towards Iran will make it impossible to coordinate its Iraq strategy with its GCC neighbours. In the present situation, the argument goes, it is unlikely that Iran could automatically expect a place at the table when the future political map of the subregion is drawn. Tehran seems to consider it prudent to keep all its options open and therefore follow a unilateralist policy towards Iraq.

These calculations are somewhat separate, however, from Tehran's more immediate concerns about Washington's intentions towards the Islamic Republic itself. There is a view in Tehran that after Saddam, Iran is likely to be the next target on the US hit list and that Tehran should be fully prepared. In this view, it would make sense for Tehran to regard

Iraq as its first line of defence and thus to find ways of ensuring that the United States does not find the time or the opportunity to attack Iran. One course would be to keep Washington fully occupied in the Levant and preoccupied with the Palestine–Israel conflict.

The military dimension with regard to Persian Gulf security is also important. The developmental agenda of the Iranian military is largely shaped by (aside from combat experience against Iraq) the Iranian navy's confrontation with the US Navy in the late 1980s, and it is informed by the performance of the American armed forces in the 1990–91 war in Kuwait and their performance in Iraq since March 2003. Back in 1990 the Pentagon's ability to apply the regional command system and bring some five hundred thousand personnel to the theatre was viewed with amazement in Tehran; American armed forces' speedy victory over Saddam Hussein's forces in 2003 merely underlined this. Iran has no illusions about the prowess of US military forces. Iran is also anxious about the US ability to deploy over-the-horizon weapons, such as cruise missiles, against Iranian targets. It would have no credible response to that method of warfare; it is therefore busy trying to find one. Above all, based on its reading of American operations, Tehran would want to avoid any direct confrontation with US armed forces in the Persian Gulf; at the same time, however, it will try to create a credible deterrent against the US Navy. This it could attempt through the deployment of advanced antiship systems and new platforms for aggressive deployment in the Gulf. Its strategy would be one of denial, based on raising the cost to the United States of naval operations against Iranian forces by attempting to block the Strait of Hormuz and harassing the Fifth Fleet.[8] Tehran has also created a three-hundred-thousand-strong 'rapid deployment force' of its own to respond to attacks on the country. A military alliance with Iraq does not, however, seem to feature in Tehran's plans.

Tehran is also worried by US proposals for a theatre-missile-defence shield around the Gulf Cooperation Council states; such a shield could support aggressive American designs, challenge Iran's defence and security, and in the meantime compromise its political relations with its GCC neighbours. In a new crisis with Iran the Gulf states might then choose a less conciliatory line. It has been said in Tehran that Iran's development and deployment of long-range ballistic missiles can be regarded as a response to the combined threats of cruise missiles and the extension of theatre missile defences to Gulf allies of the United States.

More broadly though, the place of the United States in Iran's agenda with respect to the Persian Gulf and Iraq is defined more by ideology than policy. Tehran still clearly separates its bilateral concerns with the United States from those in the US–Iraq basket. That is, this separation is favourable for the American Iraq strategy, but Iran will be immoveable as long as it sees the United States as the leader of a cultural invasion. The struggle against the United States, as no one needs reminding, plays a critical part in Iran's domestic power struggles, and as long as that remains the case, no party in Iran is likely to endorse any US action in the Persian Gulf.

Some quarters in the military of course regard the United States as an outright military threat. Brigadier General Zolqadr, the then head of the Joint Staff Command of the Sepah, regards the United States as its chief protagonist in the post-Cold War order. 'Today', he said in the mid-1990s, 'the United States is the only enemy we take as a main threat in our strategy. None of the regional countries are at a level to be a threat against Iran's security. We have organised our forces and equipment to counter the US threats and our exercises and manoeuvres have been arranged on the basis of these threats.'[9] This bold statement may not be endorsed in its entirety by Zolqadr's peers, but any action that Washington takes in the Persian Gulf subregion will automatically be interpreted by many in Tehran as part of a plot against the Islamic Republic.

The best that can be hoped for in the current climate therefore is for Tehran and Washington to continue to separate Iraq from their bilateral problems and try to ensure that their respective strategies towards Iraq do not widen and thereby encompass the other party. Iran certainly takes this view, but so long as the 'axis of evil' concept remains in the US security doctrine, the same degree of certainty cannot be expressed with regard to Washington. This is especially unfortunate, in as much as the real key to the security puzzle in the Persian Gulf is likely to be found in the future relations of Iran and Iraq with each other.

NOTES

1　Bill Samii of Radio Free Europe notes that the Iraqi culture minister Hamid Yusef Hammadi was scheduled to arrive in Tehran on 27 June 2002 for a five-day visit. Three days earlier Iraqi President Saddam Hussein cabled his counterpart condolences over the loss of life in the Iranian earthquake. The cable read: 'We express to you our heartfelt condolences on this painful incident and beseech God to have mercy upon the victims, to grant patience to their families, and protect the Iranian people from all that is evil.' *RFE/RL Iran Report*, 1 July 2002.

2　See Dilip Hiro, *Neighbours, Not Friends: Iraq and Iran after the Gulf Wars* (London: Routledge, 2001).

3　For a brief synopsis, based on US State Department sources, of the provenance and activities of this group, see Dudley Knox Library, 'Mujahedin-e Khalk Organization (MEK or MKO)', *Terrorist Group Profiles,* U.S. Naval Postgraduate School, Monterey California, library.nps.navy.mil/home.tgp/mek.htm [30 October 2002].

4　For an assessment of SCIRI, see Phebe Marr, 'Iraq the "Day After": Internal Dynamics in Post-Saddam Iraq', *Naval War College Review,* Winter 2003.

5　The three islands in dispute with the UAE are Greater Tunb Island (*Tunb al Kubra* in Arabic and *Jazireh-ye Tonb-e Bozorg* in Persian), Lesser Tunb Island (called *Tunb as Sughra* in Arabic, *Jazireh-ye Tonb-e Kuchek* in Persian) and Abu Musa (*Jazireh-ye Abu Musa* in Persian), all of which Iran has occupied or attempted to occupy.

6　Saudi Arabia may well also have agreed to supply the Iranian armed forces with spare parts for its ageing US-made hardware, and before the fall of Saddam even with Western-supplied satellite intelligence about the Iraqi armed forces.

7　*Ettela'at International,* 1 September 1997.

8　*Iran News*, 28 June 1997.

9　*Kayhan*, 10 December 1996.

Further Reading

Books

Afrasiabi, K. L., *After Khomeini: New Directions in Iran's Foreign Policy* (Boulder, Colorado: Westview Press, 1994)

Al-Suwaidi, J. S. (ed.), *Iran and the Gulf: A Search for Stability* (UAE: The Emirates Center for Strategic Studies and Research, 1996)

Amirahmadi, H. and Nader Entessar, *Iran and the Arab World* (New York: St. Martin's Press, 1993)

Bill, J. A., *The Eagle and the Lion: The Tragedy of American–Iranian Relations* (London: Yale University Press, 1988)

Calabrese, J., *Revolutionary Horizons: Regional Foreign Policy in Post-Khomeini Iran* (New York: St. Martin's Press, 1994)

Cottam, R., *Iran and the United States: A Cold War Case Study* (Pittsburgh, Pennsylvania: University of Pittsburgh Press, 1988)

Cottrell, A. J. and James E. Dougherty, *Iran's Quest for Security: U.S. Arms Transfers and the Nuclear Option* (Cambridge, Massachusetts: Institute for Foreign Policy Analysis, 1977)

Dorman, W. A. and Mansour Farhang, *The U.S. Press and Iran: Foreign Policy and the Journalism of Deference* (Berkley: University of California Press, 1987)

Ehteshami, A. and Ali Mohammadi, *Iran and Eurasia* (Reading: Ithaca Press, 2000)

Ehteshami, A. and Raymond A. Hinnebusch, *Syria and Iran: Middle Powers in a Penetrated Regional System* (London: Routledge, 1997)

Esposito, J. and Ruhollah Ramazani, *Iran at the Crossroads* (New York: Palgrave, 2001)

Everts, S., *Engaging Iran: a Test Case for EU Foreign Policy* (London: Centre for European Reform, 2004)

Ganji, B., *Politics of Confrontation: The Foreign Policy of the USA and Revolutionary Iran* (London: Tauris Academic Studies, 2006)

Gottlieb, D. M., *U.S. – Iran Foreign Policy A New Road Map* (Washington, D.C.: National Defense University, National War College, 2003)

Hiro, D., *Neighbors Not Friends: Iraq and Iran after the Gulf Wars* (London: Routledge, 2001)

Hunter, S., *Iran and the World: Continuity in a Revolutionary Decade* (Bloomington: Indiana University Press, 1990)

Kechichian, J. A., *Iran, Iraq and the Arab Gulf States* (New York: Palgrave, 2001)

Keddie, N. R., *Iran and the Muslim World: Resistance and Revolution* (New York: New York University Press, 1995)

Keddie, N. R., *Modern Iran: Roots and Results of Revolution* (Yale: Yale University Press, 2006)

Kemp, G. and Janice Gross Stein, *Powder Keg in the Middle East: the Struggle for Gulf Security* (Washington, D.C.: American Association for the Advancement of Science, 1995)

Marschall, C., *Iran's Persian Gulf Policy: From Khomeini to Khatami* (London: Routledge, 2003)

Menashri, D., *The Iranian Revolution and the Muslim World* (Boulder, Colorado: Westview Press, 1990)

Pasha, A. K., *India, Iran and the GCC States: Political Strategy and Foreign Policy* (New Delhi: Manas Publications, 2000)

Phillip, P. G., *The Islamic Republic of Iran at the United Nations: A Study of Foreign Policy Issues, 1979–1989* (Kent: University of Canterbury, 1992)

Rahnema, S. and Sohrab Behdad, *Iran after the Revolution: Crises of an Islamic State* (London: I.B. Tauris, 1995)

Ramazani, R. K., *The Foreign Policy of Iran* (Charlottesville, Virginia: University Press of Virginia, 1966)

Reissner, J., 'Europe and Iran: Critical Dialogue' in Richard N. Haass & Meghan L. O'Sullivan (eds.), *Honey and Vinegar. Incentives, Sanctions and Foreign Policy* (Washington, D.C.: Brookings Institution Press, 2000)

Rubin, B. M., *Crises in the Contemporary Persian Gulf* (London: Frank Cass, 2002)

Tarock, A., *Iran's Foreign Policy Since 1990: Pragmatism Supersedes Islamic Ideology* (New York: Nova Science Publishers, 1999)

Tekin, A., *The Place of Terrorism in Iran's Foreign Policy* (Ankara: Eurasia Center, 1998)

Vahid, R. F., *Foreign Policy of Iran* (Hamburg: University of Hamburg, 1988)

Williams, J. H., *The Ascendance of Iran: a Study of the Emergence of an Assertive Iranian* (California: U.S. Naval Postgraduate School, 1979)

Zonis, M. and Daniel Brumberg, *Khomeini, the Islamic Republic of Iran and the Arab World* (Cambridge, Massachusetts: Centre for Middle Eastern Studies, Harvard University, 1987)

Articles

Adib-Moghaddam, A., (2005) 'Islamic Utopian Romanticism and the Foreign Policy Culture of Iran', *Critique: Critical Middle Eastern Studies*, 14:3

Afrasiabi, K. and Abbas Maleki, (2003) 'Iran's Foreign Policy After 11 September', *The Brown Journal of World Affairs*, IX (2)

Halliday, F., (2001) 'Iran and the Middle East: Foreign Policy and Domestic Change', *Middle East Report*, No. 220

Hossein Razi, G. H., (1988) 'An Alternative Paradigm to State Rationality in Foreign Policy: The Iran–Iraq War', *The Western Political Quarterly*, 41 (4)

Ramazani, R. K., (2004) 'Ideology and Pragmatism in Iran's Foreign Policy', *Middle East Journal*, 58 (4)

Saidabadi, M. R., (1996) 'Islam and Foreign Policy in the Contemporary Secular World: The Case of Post-Revolutionary Iran', *Global Change, Peace & Security*, 8:2, 32–44

Shaery-Eisenlohr, R., (2007) 'Post revolutionary Iran and Shi'i Lebanon: Contested Histories of Shi'i Transnationalism", *International Journal of Middle East Studies* 39 (2)

Shaffer, B., (2003) 'Iran's Role in the South Caucasus and Caspian Region: Diverging Views of the U.S. and Europe', *SWP Berlin: Iran and its Neighbors*, July

Taheri, A., (2006) 'The World and Iran's Second Revolution', *American Foreign Policy Interests*, 28 (2)

PhDs

Al-Nahas, I.M.Y., *Continuity and Change in the Revolutionary Iran Foreign Policy: The Role of International and Domestic Political Factors in Shaping the Iranian Foreign Policy, 1979–2006* (West Virginia: West Virginia University Libraries, 2007)

Marschall, C., *The Islamic Republic of Iran and the Persian Gulf States: Iranian Regional Foreign Policy 1979–1994* (Harvard University, 1997)

Vazeri, H., *The Islamic Republic and its Neighbours: Ideology and the National Interest in Iran's Foreign Policy during the Khomeini Decade* (Georgetown University, 1995)

Index